IMAGES OF THE PAST

FALLEN IDOLS
A CENTURY OF SCREEN
SEX SCANDALS

IMAGES OF THE PAST
FALLEN IDOLS
A CENTURY OF SCREEN
SEX SCANDALS

NIGEL BLUNDELL

PEN & SWORD HISTORY

AN IMPRINT OF PEN & SWORD BOOKS LTD.
YORKSHIRE – PHILADELPHIA

First published in Great Britain in 2018 by
PEN & SWORD HISTORY
an imprint of
Pen & Sword Books Ltd,
47 Church Street,
Barnsley,
South Yorkshire
S70 2AS

A CIP record for this book is available from the British Library.

ISBN 978 1 52674 214 8

Typeset in Gill Sans 11/13 by
Aura Technology and Software Services, India
Printed and bound in India by Replika Press Pvt. Ltd.

Pen & Sword Books Limited incorporates the imprints of Atlas,
Archaeology, Aviation, Discovery, Family History, Fiction, History, Maritime,
Military, Military Classics, Politics, Select, Transport, True Crime, Air World,
Frontline Publishing, Leo Cooper, Remember When, Seaforth Publishing,
The Praetorian Press, Wharncliffe Local History, Wharncliffe Transport,
Wharncliffe True Crime and White Owl.

For a complete list of Pen & Sword titles please contact
Pen & Sword Books Limited
47 Church Street, Barnsley, South Yorkshire S70 2AS, England

E-mail: enquiries@pen-and-sword.co.uk
Website: www.pen-and-sword.co.uk

Contents

Introduction

It's a scandal! How often we use that phrase, and what a catalogue of sins it covers. Well, that is what this book is all about. It is, literally, a catalogue of sins, but committed by a very special class of culprit. They are far from being run-of-the-mill misdemeanours because they were perpetrated by some of the most celebrated names on the planet.

The transgressions crammed into this compact title all occurred during a single century when 'star status' was used to disguise extreme examples of moral lapses. Throughout the twentieth century, popular idols of screen and stage appeared to outdo each other in outraging public decency. The rules that the rest of us tried to live by appeared not to apply to them.

Why they behaved in this manner is, at first glance, a mystery. As media interest in them grew, superstars were constantly in the spotlight, their every action noted by show-business writers and gossip columnists. Yet movie stars and music icons were ready to risk every shred of respectability for a red-hot romance, a sensual soirée or a drug-fuelled dalliance.

They knew what they were doing. They were all adults. They were aware of the risks they took, the probable damage to their careers and the looming shame of exposure. So why did they persist in ignoring the pitfalls? The answer in the main is, of course, sex: the three-letter word that has spelled ignominy for so many in the world of showbiz. There were other causes of destroyed reputations, samples of which will be seen in the following chapters, but the common theme within this book is the cavalier attitude to danger and disclosure displayed by some of the biggest names to appear on screen and stage. Since so many of the twentieth-century's superstars found fame in the United States, that is from where most of these stories emanate, Hollywood not only being the heart of the film world but the hub of gossip and therefore the centre of scandal.

When the biggest glamour star of all, Marilyn Monroe, was found dead in bed there, the resulting disclosures involved drugs, mental instability, Mafia conspiracies and a procession of lovers including the president of the United States. When the dubious under-age liaisons of comics like Charlie Chaplin and Woody Allen were laid bare, the resultant backlash was no laughing matter.

Other examples of forbidden love reflect an age when 'gay' was not necessarily a description of the joys of single-sex relationships. Leading male star Rock Hudson's homosexuality was disguised by his studio bosses forcing him into a sham marriage and was revealed only when he contracted AIDS through gay orgies. Hudson's co-star in the 1956 epic *Giant*, **James Dean**, melted the hearts of young girls, and many men. The fact that he slept his way to the top with the latter came to light only after his untimely death

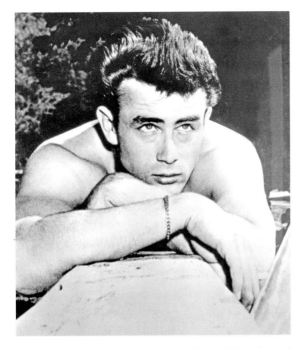

in a car crash at the age of 24. It is illuminating to examine the shock that those revelations caused at the time, yet now might be seen as evidence of sexual exploitation rather than blameworthy.

In just eighteen months, with just three major motion picture performances, Dean had become a cultural icon, but his sex life in the years leading up to his fame would have dented his career had he lived longer. In his early Hollywood days, near starving, he referred to his male dates as 'free meal tickets'. He was 'kept' by a minor producer but slept with others in Hollywood's hierarchy in the hope of being offered acting breaks. Complaining that this had not benefited him, Dean told a friend: 'I've had my cock sucked by five of the biggest names in Hollywood, and I think it's pretty funny because I wanted more than anything to get some little part; instead they'd invite me to fancy dinners.' The star of *East of Eden* and *Rebel Without a Cause* was bisexual and had affairs with actresses Pier Angeli and Ursula Andress but when asked if he was gay his reply was: 'Well, I'm certainly not going to go through life with one hand tied behind my back!'

Hollywood studios much preferred to promote their male stars' images as red-blooded hunks enjoying the charms of a string of attractive female companions. There were some, however, whose reputation was dented not by their roles as superstuds but as bedtime flops. Screen idols Errol Flynn and Clark Gable were two of those whose virility was subsequently questioned. However, the star dubbed by Hollywood as 'The Great Lover' probably bore the greatest misnomer of all. **Rudolph Valentino**'s screen image, which had women literally swooning in the aisles, was at variance with his private life, his preferred passion being for young men.

For appearance's sake, Valentino married twice, but his first wife locked him out of his

Flawed icons… James Dean (above) and Rudolph Valentino.

bedroom on his wedding night and the second treated him like a servant and made him call her 'boss'. Both women had lesbian tendencies and neither marriage was thought to have been consummated. Valentino, who worked as a cabaret dancer before rocketing to stardom in *The Four Horsemen of the Apocalypse* in 1921, bought a castle-like Hollywood mansion through which he strode in chinchilla-lined coats, dripping with gold jewellery and perfume. He was distraught when the American press taunted him for powdering his face, accusing him of 'degeneration and effeminacy'. During a promotional tour to plug his 1926 movie *The Son of the Sheik*, he suffered appendicitis and, when peritonitis set in, the 31-year-old idol sat up in his deathbed at a New York hospital and asked his doctor: 'Do I really act like a pink powder puff?'

The female equivalent of Valentino was **Clara Bow**, a superstar of the silent movies who was labelled the original 'It Girl' after appearing in the 1927 blockbuster *It*. At the age of 25, the jazz-age 'flapper' from a poverty-stricken and abusive New York upbringing was Hollywood's top sex goddess, with an off-screen lifestyle far raunchier than her comparatively tame and highly-censored screen portrayals of the time. Her nemesis came in the form of her private secretary, Daisy DeVoe, whom she rightly sued for embezzling $16,000. The resultant court case rebounded when Daisy revealed Clara's bedroom antics, including affairs with actors Gary Cooper, Eddie Cantor and Bela Lugosi. Although sentenced to jail for eighteen months, Daisy added to Clara's torment by selling further revelations to a scandal sheet, with a description

Secret lovers… 'It Girl' Clara Bow and the young John Wayne.

of the actress giving herself to an entire football team, including a young Marion Morrison, later to become **John Wayne**. Clara lost her studio contract with Paramount and had a nervous breakdown, the first of many.

The woman who replaced Clara Bow as Paramount's leading lady was the notorious **Mae West**. Despite her reputation, she was discreet about the many men in her life; the scandals she caused were all well-rehearsed. Her most famous lines were:

Courting controversy… magnificent Mae West.

'I used to be Snow White but I drifted', 'Between two evils, I always try the one I've never tried before', 'When I'm good I'm very good but when I'm bad I'm better' and most famously, though misquoted, 'Come up and see me some time'. (In fact, her invitation to Cary Grant in the 1933 comedy *She Done Him Wrong* was: 'Come up some time, see me.') That film is known as a 'Pre-Code' movie because it was produced in the brief period between the introduction of talkies and the full enforcement of censorship on the American cinema under the aegis of chief enforcer Will Hays. Mae West's sexual innuendo prompted Hays to depute a censor to stay on the set of her next film, *Belle of the Nineties*. Its original title had been *It Ain't No Sin* but it had to be changed after lobbying by the Roman Catholic Church and picketing by priests with posters proclaiming: 'Yes It Is'!

The so-called Hays Code reflected the increasingly censorious approach to the perceived immorality and decadent influence of Hollywood. The code's overriding principle was that 'No picture shall be produced that will lower the moral standards of those who see it.' It was developed into a series of rules covering, among many others: Crimes Against The Law, Sex, Vulgarity, Obscenity, Profanity and 'Repellent Subjects'. The code not only affected what was portrayed on screen, however. The rules laid down by Will Hays, backed by similar strictures of the influential Catholic Legion of Decency, influenced the private lives of the players themselves.

Scandalously, one of the code's unpublicized effects was to make abortion almost a form of birth control. Hays had persuaded studios to introduce mandatory 'morality clauses' into stars' contracts. Thus an unintended pregnancy would not only shame an actress, but would violate studio policy. Throughout the 1930s, stars such as Tallulah Bankhead 'got abortions like other women got permanent waves', according to her biographer Lee Israel. In the same decade, Jean Harlow's romance with married co-star William Powell resulted in MGM booking her for an 'appendectomy' in the same private hospital into which a year later, under the name 'Mrs Jean Carpenter', she was again admitted 'to get some rest'. MGM's publicity chief Howard Strickling also handled the 'embarrassment' of musical star Jeanette MacDonald's pregnancy after studio boss Louis B. Mayer told him to 'get rid of the problem'. MacDonald was checked into hospital with an 'ear infection'. Strickling similarly arranged a termination for Joan Crawford who, while estranged from husband Douglas Fairbanks Jr, became pregnant with what she believed was Clark Gable's child. Crawford's rival **Bette Davis** also chose to have abortions for the sake of her career. As she readily admitted late in life, having a child in 1934 would have made her 'miss the biggest role in my life thus far', as Mildred in *Of Human Bondage*.

Such was the power of the Hays Code that, in many ways, it stifled creativity in American cinema for three decades until the 1960s when a new certification was introduced by the Motion Picture Association of America. What it failed to do was prevent the off-screen activities of the actors and actresses themselves. It did, however, make the revelations of their freewheeling lifestyles appear even more scandalous if and when they were eventually exposed to public opprobrium.

Over the decades, there has been no shortage of those who would kiss-and-tell and those who would listen. More than half a century ago, gossip columnists like rivals Hedda Hopper and Louella Parsons were nationally syndicated and read weekly by 50 million avid US fans. In more recent times, supermarket magazines and newspaper tabloids on both sides of the Atlantic have fed the public the celebrity coverage they crave.

The biggest blockbusters have often come in book form, of course, and when stars suffer by the poison of the pen, it is at its most damaging when wielded by a member of the subject's own family. Most famously, screen goddess Joan Crawford's reputation was comprehensively trashed by her adopted daughter's 1978 biography, mockingly titled *Mommie Dearest*. The nightmare portrayal of life with a viciously abusive mother is related elsewhere in this book. A similar posthumous act of character assassination was performed on one of the movies' best-loved musical stars, 'Old Groaner' **Bing Crosby**.

Following Bing's death in 1977, his son Gary, one of four boys by his first wife, actress Dixie Lee, painted a picture of a cold, cruel parent. In his book *Going My Own Way*, he said his father beat him and his brothers with a leather belt and humiliated him by calling him 'stupid' and 'fatso'. Gary blamed his father for his alcoholism and for youngest brother

Secret abortions… Bette Davis.

Trashed reputations… Bing Crosby.

Lindsay's nervous breakdown. Friends were seldom invited to the Crosby home, said Gary, because Bing did not want them to see what he was really like with his family.

Supporting evidence came from the sons' nanny Eve Kelly, who said: 'All they wanted from their father was love but they never got it. He tried to drill into me that I should punish the children on Wednesdays for all the things they had done wrong during the week. But I couldn't do that. It didn't seem fair.' Even one of Bing's closest friends, his authorized biographer Charles Thompson, revealed some unsavoury home truths. He said that Bing's second marriage to actress Kathryn Grant was always stormy and was on the verge of breaking up when he died. He also told of the wealthy singer's penny-pinching meanness and his coldness towards his children, whom he often caned, Bing having once told him: 'Maybe I didn't lay into them with a belt as often as I should have done.'

Biographies such as that have regularly reduced their subject's stature, as happened to Crosby's co-star in *High Society*, the equally fan-favoured Grace Kelly. Princess Grace of Monaco, as she became, was the epitome of upper-crust gentility, yet, as will be detailed in a later chapter, her subjects were shocked when her sexual shenanigans were revealed after her death in a car crash in 1982.

Like Kelly, British actress **Vivien Leigh** was the child of a wealthy, well-connected couple and her screen roles were a natural reflection of her real-life genteel breeding as a young English rose. She went on to capture the world as Scarlett O'Hara in *Gone with the Wind* and she married one of the world's greatest-ever actors, Laurence Olivier.

Warring couple… Vivien Leigh and Laurence Olivier were a tempestuous double-act.

However, her legend was shattered by a series of grievous revelations following her death from tuberculosis at the age of 53 in 1967. Lord Olivier himself confirmed his wife's nymphomania and her one-night stands with low-class pick-ups. Her most tempestuous affair, however, was with actor Peter Finch, whose first wife Tamara she drunkenly tried to stab with a pair of scissors during a Hollywood reception. The affair ended after two years with a confrontation between her husband and Finch at the Oliviers' English country home. After dinner, the two men went into the library to try to resolve the triangle. Suddenly Vivien threw open the door and said: 'Will one of you come to bed with me now?' Finch left the house and promised never to see the actress again. Vivien's violent outbursts increased until Olivier finally left her 'because I was afraid of killing her'.

Such public spats made the juiciest of screen idol scandals, mostly tapped out by star-chasing scribblers, and there is nothing that gossip columnists love more than a feud between celebrities. After all, they get two star names in a paragraph for the price of one! Hollywood's most infamous falling-out was between Joan Crawford and Bette Davis, both employed in the 1940s by Warner Bros, where they had adjoining dressing rooms. Their bitchiness became legendary, each briefing against the other, criticizing their rival backgrounds, roles and love lives. In 1962 the pair agreed to play opposite each other as warring sisters in the psychological thriller *What Ever Happened to Baby Jane?* Despite having equal billing, the stage was set for the snidest snub of all.

In the run-up to the following year's Oscars ceremony, Crawford was outraged that her co-star was hot favourite to win the Best Actress award, while she had not even been nominated. Davis already had two Oscars and a third would have made her the first actress in Hollywood history to collect a trio. Crawford retaliated by launching a behind-the-scenes campaign to persuade members of the Academy of Motion Picture Arts and Sciences to 'vote for anyone but Davis'. She then volunteered to act as a stand-in for any nominees unable to attend on the night. As the nominations were read out, Davis stubbed out her cigarette and handed her purse to a friend, ready to collect her expected trophy, but was shocked to hear not her name but that of Anne Bancroft as Best Actress for the biopic *The Miracle Worker*. Davis was even more stunned when Crawford pushed past her, saying: 'Excuse me, I have an Oscar to collect.' Her rival then gloatingly walked up to accept the award, stealing her limelight. To quote Hedda Hopper in her next column: 'When it comes to giving or stealing a show, nobody can top Joan Crawford.'

An earlier public Oscar upset had been the result of a family feud between sisters Olivia de Havilland and Joan Fontaine. In 1942 both found themselves nominated for Best Actress: de Havilland for the romantic comedy *Hold Back the Dawn* and Fontaine for the Alfred Hitchcock thriller *Suspicion*. Fontaine won, which might explain why five years later, after winning the Oscar herself for *To Each His Own*, de Havilland gave her younger sister the cold shoulder when she went over to congratulate her.

A rather more serious split involved high-living actor **Kiefer Sutherland** and *Pretty Woman* star Julia Roberts, who were all set to be married in the most talked-about wedding Hollywood had seen in years. The bill was to be a cool $1 million and 500 of the industry's top stars and moguls were due to attend. Then, at the last minute, Sutherland saw his hopes of marrying his Pretty Woman flounder because of his continued trysts, particularly his relationship with a nightclub dancer called Amanda Rice. Roberts wrought her revenge by dumping her unruly groom only three days before the 1992 wedding. Sutherland reacted by going on another bender. Amanda retaliated by blabbing to the press that

Secret tryst… Kiefer Sutherland.

Miserable mugshots... Hugh Grant and Divine Brown.

Sutherland had told her: 'Making love to Julia was like having sex with a corpse!'

Astonishingly, some stars who would not normally have trouble attracting sex partners have chosen instead to pay for their pleasures. Handsome **Hugh Grant**'s miserable mugshot flashed around the world after Los Angeles police booked him for lewd conduct with prostitute Divine Brown. In 1995 the British actor had cruised the city's Sunset Boulevard in his BMW before picking up the hooker and parking in a side-street while she performed oral sex on him for the sum of $60. On his release, Grant said: 'Last night I did something completely insane. I have hurt people I love and embarrassed people I work with. For both those things I am more sorry than I can ever possibly say.' Divine Brown gave a blow-by-blow account of her side of the story, revealing that Grant had told her: 'I always wanted to have sex with a black woman; that's my fantasy.'

The high price of hookers... Charlie Sheen.

The $60 that Hugh Grant paid for side-street sex would have been small change to **Charlie Sheen**, who admitted paying $53,500 over two years for romps with prostitutes. His confession came in a video link during the 1995 money-laundering trial of 'Hollywood Madam' Heidi Fleiss, whose call girls he paid up to $3,000 a time on at least twenty-seven occasions, including on Christmas Day 1992. At the end of the hearing, he said: 'I apologize to my family, my future wife and my close friends of the embarrassment these incidents may have caused.' The star of the 1986 movie *Platoon* went on to become the highest-paid actor on TV, earning $1.8million per episode of *Two and a Half Men*. However, his humility at the Fleiss hearing proved false when he was more recently shamed as a sex addict who had been tested as HIV positive.

Like Charlie Sheen, former teen idol **Rob Lowe** was a 1980s film star who turned to TV, then saw his career falter because of a sex scandal. Lowe's sizzling one-night stand with a nightclub entertainer during the Democratic Convention in Atlanta, Georgia in 1988 made tabloid headlines. Jan Parsons was just 16 years of age when she ended up in bed with Lowe and another girl, their steamy sex session captured forever on video. 'It was one of those quirky, naughty wild sort of drunken things that people do from time to time,' said Lowe, then aged 24. When the video came to light and was flashed around the world, Lowe was arraigned and punished for his misdeeds with twenty hours of community service. Jan Parsons faded from the scene; so too for a while did Lowe, as his superstar status unsurprisingly stalled.

'Naughty drunken things' could be the description of several of the silver screen's once shining stars. The comedian **W.C. Fields** was famous for his one-liners, one of the most apposite being: 'A woman drove me to drink and I didn't even have the decency to thank her.' Rarely seen without a glass in his hand, his final major role was playing his spirits-swilling self in the 1941 movie *Never Give a Sucker an Even Break*. Fields seemed quite happy to drink himself to death, which he managed to do on Christmas Day 1946.

Buster Keaton was another comedian whose most notable work was conducted while inebriated. The man once considered an equal to Charlie Chaplin had boozy blackouts lasting days, which caused MGM to drop him in 1933. Leading man **William Holden** enjoyed acting acclaim but died in 1981 after falling over drunk in his apartment and bleeding to death from a head wound. Suave **Gig Young** played an alcoholic in the 1951 James Cagney movie *Come Fill the Cup* and won a Best Supporting Actor Oscar in 1969 for *They Shoot Horses, Don't They?* A lifelong alcoholic, he shot his wife and then himself in his New York apartment in 1978.

Drunken sex romp… Rob Lowe.

Drunk on the film set… W.C. Fields.

Boozy blackouts… Buster Keaton (above) was fired and William Holden died.

A mixture of booze and hard drugs wrecked the life of **Richard Pryor**, regarded as one of the greatest stand-up comedians of all time until his smoking, snorting and injecting almost killed him. He was married seven times to five women amid bitter allegations of violence. 'I dulled my pain with drugs to loosen up and make people laugh,' he said. However, in 1980 while freebasing cocaine during the making of the film *Stir Crazy*, he went one step too far by pouring rum over his body before setting himself alight. Police found Pryor running from his Los Angeles home with his whole body ablaze. He survived second- and third-degree burns but, later diagnosed with multiple sclerosis, died of a heart attack in 2005.

Another star who seemed to have a death wish was actress **Frances Farmer**, who director Howard Hawks praised as 'having more talent than anyone I ever worked with'. After starring in *Come and Get It* in 1936, her daily cocktail of booze and pills unhinged her and she spent ten years in mental institutions. All-action hero **Alan Ladd** was traumatized after witnessing his alcoholic mother die in convulsions after eating rat poison. Ladd, whose greatest role was in the 1953 Western *Shane*, also turned to the bottle, dying in 1964 after swilling a mixture of sedatives and alcohol. **George Sanders**, who so memorably portrayed screen villains in movies such as the 1940 cliffhanger *Rebecca*, took a barbiturate overdose in a Spanish hotel in 1972. **Judy Garland**, *The Wizard of Oz* child star turned tortured singer, was found dead in the bathroom of her rented London house in 1969, the coroner giving the cause of death as 'an incautious overdose of barbiturates'. Other posthumous pill-poppers included, of course, Marilyn Monroe and Elvis Presley, whose tragic denouements are related in subsequent chapters.

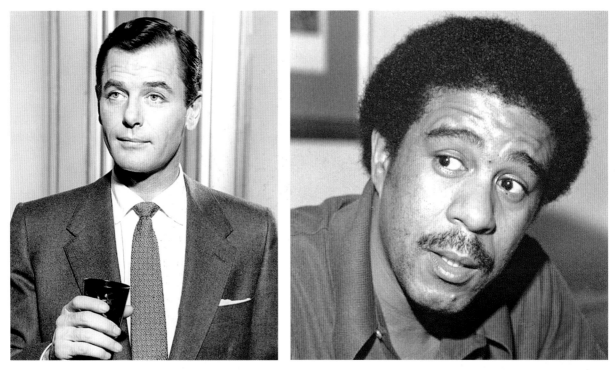

Death wish… Gig Young (left) shot himself and Richard Prior set himself alight.

Talent tainted by a cocktail of booze and pills… Frances Farmer and Alan Ladd.

Stars who took deadly overdoses… George Sanders and Judy Garland.

Again, the lesson learned from these famous cases of celebrity scandal (though often, it seems, not by the celebrities themselves!) is that the bigger the star, the harder they fall. Their careers may have been stellar, but the proclivities they tried to hide ultimately led to gossip, exposure and shame. On the following pages are some of the most startling scandals of the twentieth century. They reflect an age when the headlines were at their most shocking, saucy, salacious and sensational, and when deceit and intrigue so often turned hard-won fame into instant infamy.

CHAPTER ONE

Charlie Chaplin

To his millions of fans, Charlie Chaplin was the greatest silent movie actor of all time. His blend of clowning and pathos marked him out as comic genius and his dark, soulful eyes had women swooning wherever his films were shown. Those who saw classics such as *Easy Street*, *The Immigrant* and *The Kid* believed in the 'little Tramp' and his crazy adventures. He was the hapless, the harmless, the victim, the innocent.

Yet Chaplin's private life was increasingly dissected and devoured by a scandal-hungry press. The tramp, it seemed, had penchants for threesomes, fellatio and performing intercourse in front of spectators. Above all, he liked sex with schoolgirls.

Born into an impoverished London family on 16 April 1889, Charles Spencer Chaplin had arrived in America from their native Britain with the Fred Karno vaudeville troupe in 1912. He was just 23, shy, lonely and inexperienced with women. In Hollywood, however, he swiftly developed a potent sex life, with a particular penchant for young girls.

In 1917 a child actress caught his eye: 15-year-old Mildred Harris, to whom he promised a glittering future in the movies. The naïve child was won over and a year later she announced that she was pregnant. Chaplin hurriedly married her, although the pregnancy turned out to be a false alarm. Mildred subsequently did give birth to a son, tragically deformed; he died just three days old. The marriage ended in divorce in 1920, with Chaplin accusing his young bride of adultery and she accusing him of cruelty.

Chaplin's next conquest was Lillita MacMurray, another child star whose career Chaplin had followed intently since meeting her at the age of 6. He placed her in his movies *The Kid* and *The Gold Rush* and it was while being screen-tested for a promised lead role in the latter that he first tried to seduce her. She was just 15; he was 34. She later revealed that he had put his hand up her skirt in the back of his car, curtained from the chauffeur's view, but her scream stopped him going further. On another occasion, he tried to molest her in his hotel room. She said: 'He kissed my mouth and neck and his fingers darted over my body. His body writhed furiously against mine, and suddenly some of my fright gave way to revulsion.' In another hotel room, he peeled off her clothes and stared at her naked body for several minutes before she fled. Eventually, Chaplin succeeded in taking her virginity in the steam room of his Hollywood mansion while her chaperone waited outside.

Lillita MacMurray, who liked to be called 'Lolita', changed her name to Lita Grey and it was under that name that Chaplin married her in 1924, but again only under duress after the girl, who had just turned 17, announced that she was pregnant. Chaplin, who had never used any form of contraception, was nevertheless horrified. He ordered her to have an abortion, but she refused. He then offered her $20,000 to marry someone else. He even tried to cajole the girl into committing suicide. It took the threat of a paternity suit and a charge of statutory rape to make the star marry Lita.

Though that union produced sons Charles and Sydney, the marriage again spun into trouble. During her 1926 legal action, Lita revealed how her husband had sex with at least five mistresses during the marriage, how he tried to talk her into a bedroom threesome, how he wanted them to copulate in front of an audience and how he would threaten her with a loaded revolver. One of her accusations was that he had asked her to perform 'the abnormal, against nature, perverted, degenerate and indecent act' of fellatio and that, when she refused, he had assured her: 'Relax, dear. All married people do it!'

The star eventually made a $625,000 settlement on Lita and their children after a threat by her to reveal to the world the names of the five famous women she said

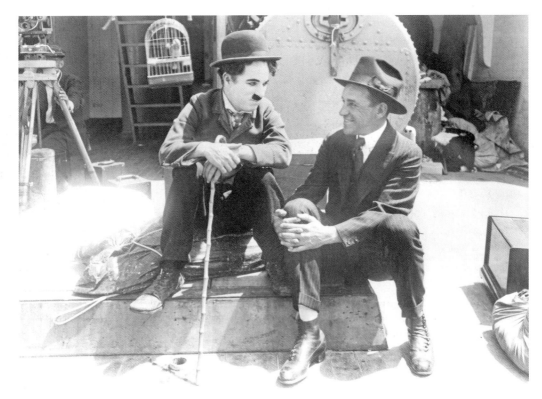

Charlie Chaplin with his studio manager on the set of *The Immigrant* in 1917.

he had made love to during their marriage. Lita poured more opprobrium on her ex-husband in an autobiography, *My Life With Chaplin*, in which she revealed the full extent of his unhealthy appetite for young girls. She said he was sexually fascinated by them, adding: 'He liked to cultivate them, to gain their trust, to be their first, never their second, lover. He believed that the most beautiful form of life was a very young girl just starting to bloom.' He once told Lita: 'Some Mr Novembers can be disgusting when they're with some Miss Mays, eager to corrupt innocence. I'm not like that. God knows that I'm not.' Once, when Lita commented that he could have his pick of any one of a hundred women in two minutes, Charlie replied: 'A hundred? No, a thousand. But I want to be naughty with you, not with them.'

That may have been merely a boast. The comedian was by now one of the world's most famous faces. For years, he had been hero-worshipped and attracted what would now be termed 'groupies', revelling in the attentions of the youngest among them. He would deflower them during studio breaks 'in that hour when I am bored'. He did not restrict his romantic adventures to the young, however. He had, it was said, pursued and seduced many notable women including Winston Churchill's cousin Clare Sheridan, Ziegfeld girl Peggy Hopkins Joyce and actresses Mabel Normand, Edna Purviance, Pola Negri and Marion Davies. As a prelude to passion, he would recite to them erotic passages from *Fanny Hill* and *Lady Chatterley's Lover*.

It was said that Chaplin had also used prostitutes as a distraction in his highly-active sex life and that he was a voyeur, having set up a telescope at his house to peer into his neighbour John Barrymore's bedroom. 'No art can be learned at once,' he told friends. 'And lovemaking is a sublime art that needs

A suave young Chaplin and his first teenaged bride Mildred Harris.

practice if it is to be true and significant.' The sex-mad movie king was supposedly able to have sex six times in succession with only a few minutes rest in between. He was proud of his technique and referred to his well-endowed manhood as 'the eighth wonder of the world'.

Chaplin in his 1921 hit *The Kid*.

The Hollywood gossip writers had a field day with all this, of course. Which is why, suffering the publicity that surrounded his divorce from Lita Grey, Chaplin kept his third match masked in secrecy. Indeed, there is no proof that this latest 'marriage' was legal. Chaplin wed 20-year-old starlet Paulette Goddard in a mysterious ceremony said to have taken place either aboard his yacht *Panacea* in 1934 or on an oriental cruise in 1936, after which the couple lived as husband and wife at his Beverly Hills home. Goddard appears to have been more strong-willed than his previous spouses and enjoyed success independently of Chaplin, although two of her most notable roles were as the female lead in his last silent film *Modern Times* in 1936 and in his first talkie *The Great Dictator* in 1940. When their relationship fizzled out, they obtained a 'quickie divorce' in Mexico in 1942.

Hardly had that match ended than the scandal for which Chaplin became notorious broke in the press. In 1943 an ambitious 22-year-old actress called Joan Barry alleged that, having bedded her from the age of 15, she was now carrying his love child. The star, then aged 53, was not only facing a paternity suit but a federal anti-prostitution charge that he had transported a minor across state lines for immoral purposes.

Barry claimed Chaplin had promised to make her a leading lady and paid for her to receive singing and acting lessons. Even after the relationship turned sour, they had indulged their lust in the most bizarre ways. Barry claimed that at Christmas 1942 she forced her way into his home pointing a gun at him. The incident aroused the couple's sense of eroticism and they had sex in the bedroom. However, he pressed charges and she was given a thirty-day jail sentence for unlawfully entering his house.

On her release, Barry poured out the whole sordid story to Hollywood's most notorious gossip columnist, Hedda Hopper. The scandal scribbler had long loathed Chaplin for his rumoured liaisons with minors, his renowned left-wing and Russian sympathies and his dogged refusal to seek full American citizenship. Now she had the ammunition she needed to vilify him in public. She ran a series of articles suggesting that Chaplin was the father of Joan Barry's unborn child. He responded by putting off a proposed marriage to his fourth wife, the 17-year-old Oona O'Neill, and embarked on a damage limitation exercise to try to salve his reputation. It failed. In June 1943, Barry filed her paternity suit.

Before it could be heard, however, Chaplin had to fight the FBI prosecution alleging that he had brought Barry across state boundaries to New York specifically to have intercourse with her. He hired leading lawyer Jerry Giesler, unofficial attorney-to-the-stars, who turned in his usual masterly performance. He argued that Charlie and Joan had enjoyed a private romance and that it was at no time necessary for him to ferry her around the country for sex. The jury agreed and Chaplin walked free, but now his reputation was permanently tarnished. Public sympathy was running against him.

Joan's child, Carol Ann, was born in October 1943 and she milked every ounce of publicity she could out of the event. When the paternity suit at last came to court the following year, she ensured that Carol Ann was with her every day. In the eyes of the jury, this undoubtedly promoted her case as a lone mother abandoned by a heartless, wealthy film star. They were also impressed by the firebrand prosecutor who referred to Chaplin in court as 'a runt of a Svengali' and a 'lecherous hound'.

Chaplin's second teenaged bride, Lita Grey, with whom he had two children.

Charmer Chaplin in the 1931 film *City Lights*.

Chaplin's third bride Paulette Goddard.

Yet blood tests carried out on Chaplin showed that he was not the child's father. His lawyers argued that Joan had indulged in affairs with at least one other man during her relationship with Charlie. Some of her travelling expenses, it was claimed, had been met by the oil tycoon J. Paul Getty. The inference was clear but was not backed by a shred of proof. It seemed Chaplin had escaped, but in a weird judicial twist, the court decided that he should pay a substantial undisclosed sum towards the child's maintenance.

Public opinion held that this was the very least the star should expect. Continuing rumours about his red-under-the-bed tendencies and hints that he was a tax evader prompted outrage among patriotic Americans. Many boycotted his 1947 film *Monsieur Verdoux* and, though it was hailed an artistic triumph by the critics, it was a financial flop. Chaplin began to see that he would not easily be forgiven for his indiscretions.

In 1952 he left the US for a holiday in Switzerland with Oona, whom he had married in 1943. He probably knew that his re-entry to America would be challenged by the government and made no attempt to return. Instead he declared himself a 'citizen of the world' and made a permanent residence in Switzerland. He returned to the US only once, in 1972, to receive an honorary Oscar in recognition of his contribution to the movie business. He got another Academy Award the following year for his score of *Limelight*, released in 1952.

Charlie Chaplin died in 1977 and Oona in 1991, leaving eight children. Of Joan Barry, little was heard after she was committed to a Californian mental hospital in 1953. She died in obscurity in New York in 2007.

In 1940 Chaplin wrote, directed, produced, scored and starred in *The Great Dictator*.

Actress Joan Barry, with lawyer Jerry Giesler, claimed Chaplin bedded her aged 15.

The 17-year-old Oona O'Neill was Chaplin's final and longest-lasting love. They wed in 1943 and lived in Switzerland until his death at the age of 88 on Christmas Day 1977. Even in old age (he is pictured left aged 82), Chaplin was still troubled by historic accusations of sex abuse.

CHAPTER TWO

Fatty Arbuckle

Charlie Chaplin may have been one of the biggest names in Hollywood but Roscoe 'Fatty' Arbuckle was at one time bigger. An astute businessman as well as a movie icon, in the early days of silent movie-making his star status was higher than Chaplin's and, that being the case, his downfall was swifter.

Arbuckle's disgrace was all the more scandalous because it was so public. It happened at a party he was throwing in 1921 to celebrate his signing of a new studio contract. The bash at a luxurious San Francisco hotel was into its third day and the booze was still flowing as still more guests arrived. Yet due to the host's sexual excesses that morning, the career of 20-stone Fatty Arbuckle would soon be in ruins. Disgraced and vilified, he would be run out of Hollywood, never again able to work under his own name.

Born in Kansas on 24 March 1887, Roscoe Conkling Arbuckle started his working life as a plumber's mate. His first experience of acting came at small-town carnivals before he progressed to the stages of vaudeville and, by the age of 21, was working as a film extra in Hollywood. Arbuckle was hardly the classic shape for a movie actor, but his physical attributes got him noticed. Although he had a huge frame of 320lb, he was surprisingly nimble on his feet, a combination which, along with his angelic expressions and schoolboy features, made him naturally funny.

In 1910 he got a leading role in *The Sanitarium*, the movie that launched him into the big time. He signed with mogul Joseph Schenck to work for the then-incredible sum of $5,000 a week, plus 25 per cent of the profits and complete artistic control. It meant that not

Temptation… but Fatty Arbuckle was known among starlets as a 'brotherly' and 'protective' figure.

only was he starring in films but writing and directing them, with classics such as *Fatty's Day Off*, *A Quiet Little Wedding* and *The Masquerader*.

Fun-loving and hard-drinking, Arbuckle was genuinely popular in Tinseltown. With his kind of influence, he could have made full use of the casting couch, yet he seems to have rarely made a pass at the bright young things he worked with. Several of them described him as 'brotherly' and 'protective' in his attitude towards them. He certainly had nothing like the Romeo reputation of Charlie Chaplin.

By 1921 Roscoe was a multi-millionaire, thanks to a deal with Paramount Pictures to work for three years for $3 million, a fabulous sum in those days. He decided to celebrate with a party, the like of which California had seldom seen. That was his downfall. He and several carloads of his merry-making pals drove 400 miles from Los Angeles to occupy three suites that the comedian had hired at the luxurious Hotel St Francis. The party began on the night of 3 September 1921, the Saturday evening of Labor Day weekend. Fuelled by several cases of bootleg booze, it went on through Sunday and into Monday. At mid-morning on Monday, as most of the revellers lay in a drunken stupor, four pretty young actresses turned up and the party roared back to life.

One of the newcomers was a starlet named Virginia Rappe, who Arbuckle had long fancied. He had initially been attracted by her cherubic appearance, which was deceptive because Virginia was anything but virtuous. During her employment with Mack Sennett's film company, so the story goes, she slept around so much that production was disrupted when several of the staff needed treatment for crabs. One person she did not fancy sleeping with, however, was Fatty Arbuckle. She had previously told friends that she found him 'unattractive' and had vowed: 'I'd sooner go to bed with a jungle ape than have that fat octopus groping at me.'

If Fatty knew about Virginia's promiscuous past and her opinion of him, it didn't seem to bother him. Perhaps he knew that the sheer clout he carried in Hollywood would be sufficient to talk her into his bed. He had specifically asked his friend Bambina Maude Delmont to invite her along. Both women were staying at the nearby Palace Hotel with Virginia's agent, Al Semnacher. When Virginia arrived, Arbuckle was still in his pyjamas, slippers and bathrobe. They did not meet immediately and it wasn't until she had been handed her third gin and orange and was complaining to other guests that the

Arbuckle's image was a picture of innocence.

bathroom seemed constantly occupied that Arbuckle whirled into view. He grabbed her by the arm and, with a conspiratorial wink to friends, shepherded her towards the nearest bedroom. Several guests heard him say: 'This is what I have been waiting for.'

About five minutes later the hubbub of noise in the main suite was abruptly silenced by piercing screams from one of the bedrooms. Maude Delmont grabbed the door of room 1219 and, finding it locked, shouted: 'Virginia, what's happening?' The screaming persisted and in desperation Maude called the hotel manager. Hardly had he got to the door than it burst open and out stepped an amused-looking Arbuckle. He grinned, performed a tap dance on the carpet and tilted Virginia's hat to a drunken angle on his head. Behind him in the room Virginia's groaning was still audible and the sound seemed to irritate Fatty. 'Get her dressed and take her back to the Palace,' he snapped at Maude. When Virginia began

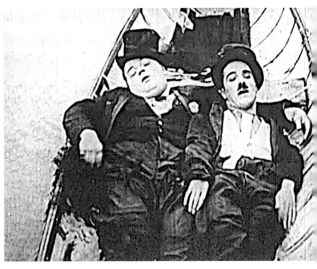

Arbuckle smartly dressed in studio pose (left) and as a dishevelled drunk, alongside Chaplin in their 1914 film *The Rounders*.

screaming again, he turned his venom on her, warning: 'Shut up or I'll throw you out of the window.' The poor girl took no notice, complaining: 'I'm dying, I'm dying. He hurt me.'

Virginia was almost naked and it was difficult to get her dressed. Her badly-ripped blouse had been torn off her body. Arbuckle seemed oblivious to the drama. His dismissive attitude left guests in no doubt that he suspected Virginia of 'putting it on'; maybe even to influence him into giving her a good part. 'Shut up,' he bellowed at her again. 'You always were a lousy actress.'

Three days later Virginia died of peritonitis. An autopsy showed that her full bladder had burst, an injury that may have occurred when Arbuckle threw his bulk on top of her. The newspapers immediately spoke of him as a sex fiend who held orgies as a matter of course and was guilty of rape. There were untrue rumours that his manhood was so large that it had penetrated Virginia's bladder in the act of intercourse. Arbuckle's friend Al Semnacher fuelled even wilder gossip by suggesting that the star had pushed a large ice cube up her vagina and sexually assaulted her with a champagne bottle.

An inquest decided that Arbuckle was 'criminally responsible' for her death and he was later charged with manslaughter. In the eyes of his public he was already guilty. Church leaders demanded a ban on his films, women's groups expressed outrage and in Wyoming a group of cowboys peppered a movie screen with bullets because it was showing a Fatty film.

At his trial in November 1921 Arbuckle angrily refuted the charge against him. His lawyers claimed that Virginia Rappe was little more than a common whore who'd had several abortions and venereal diseases. They got most of the jury on his side, but the majority vote of ten to two in Fatty's favour was insufficient to get an acquittal. A new trial was held in which jurors concluded just the opposite, voting ten to two that he was guilty. Eventually, he was cleared at the third attempt. The jury foreman told the judge: 'Acquittal is not enough. We feel a grave injustice has been done to him and there is not the slightest proof to connect him in any way with the commission of a crime.'

Arbuckle emerged from court to tell reporters: 'My innocence of the

Two images portraying Virginia Rappe as a young innocent. The truth was very different.

Virginia Rappe in a more suggestive pose… and police mugshots of her alleged attacker.

hideous charge preferred against me has been proved.' It was a statement delivered more out of bravado than any real conviction. The mud had stuck and Fatty's public could no longer laugh at him. His career was in tatters and his newly-signed $3 million contract was torn up.

No one had emerged from the trials with credit. Virginia Rappe was exposed as having been a virtual call girl, had been pregnant and suffering from venereal disease. Arbuckle, who had showed no remorse throughout, was revealed as a lecher and a drunk, and studio bosses were shamed by revelations that four years earlier Arbuckle and movie executives had attended a similarly orgiastic party that had been hushed up.

A 'Clean Up Hollywood' committee was formed by the studios, and Arbuckle was banned from working. His producer Mack Sennett had the studios fumigated. Paramount buried new, unscreened films previously made by the comic. Actors were made to sign contractual clauses promising to behave decently. Censorship was introduced and a strict code of morality for films was laid down.

Arbuckle's career was washed out (as in this still from his 1918 film *Night Nurse*) following the damaging press coverage of his scandalous court case.

ARBUCKLE INDICTED FOR MANSLAUGHTER IN ACTRESS' DEATH

Grand Jury Acts After Two Hearings—Mrs. Delmont Tells of Hotel Tragedy.

SAYS VICTIM ACCUSED HIM

Admits She Herself Had Ten Drinks of Whisky, Danced and Wore Man's Pajamas.

UNDUE INFLUENCE CHARGED

Prosecutor Says Witnesses Are Being Tampered With and Believes One Is Perjurer.

SAN FRANCISCO, Sept. 13 —The Grand Jury late tonight returned an indictment of manslaughter in the case of Roscoe (" Fatty ") Arbuckle, accused of causing the death of Miss Virginia Rappe.

The vote of the grand jurors, it was reported, was twelve to two for a manslaughter indictment.

Arbuckle with his lawyers, who finally won the star's acquittal, yet he never worked again.

Arbuckle himself had to sell his house and prized fleet of limousines and vintage cars in order to pay his lawyers' fees. A studio ban on his appearance in movies, which had originally been for eight months, was extended indefinitely and he was never able to work again under his own name. Fatty's old friend Buster Keaton is believed to have bankrolled him and to have sought roles for him in a couple of minor movies under the name of William B. Goodrich or, ironically, 'Will B. Goode' for short. For the next ten years, however, the fallen star lived the life of a second-string actor, touring small provincial theatres. In one interview for *Photoplay* magazine he begged: 'Just let me work. I think I can entertain and gladden the people that see me.'

Finally, in June 1933, at the age of 46, he seized his comeback chance. Warner Brothers signed him to make a series of comedy shorts and, with some trepidation, a celebration party was thrown at a hotel in New York. The bash ended with another tragic death. They found Fatty Arbuckle in his room, the victim of a massive coronary.

CHAPTER THREE

Jean Harlow

A sex scandal without sex sounds like a contradiction in terms. Yet in Hollywood normality is often turned on its head, and when a rich and powerful studio executive killed himself within two months of marrying one of the most famously beautiful actresses on the silver screen, the result was an unprecedented storm of rumour, blame, outrage and, ultimately, humiliation.

The actress involved was Jean Harlow, the first real sex goddess of the 'talkies' whose career path from obscurity to superstardom was spectacular, though not without controversy. Born Harlean Harlow Carpenter on 3 March 1911 in Kansas City, she was the only child of a respected dentist. Her mother Jean Harlow Carpenter divorced and, sadly for Jean, it was not her loving father who became the influence on her life but her grasping, sex-mad stepfather Marino Bello, a con-man with gangster connections.

Bello was happy to see his stepdaughter displaying her charms, to the shock of the family's respectable peers. When, as a 15-year-old, she was reprimanded for her sexy image, she told her teacher: 'I can't breathe when I'm wearing a brassiere.' All signs pointed to a girl of sexual precocity, and it was rumoured that her Svengali-like stepfather was her secret lover. She certainly remained under the unhealthy influence of him and her mother when the family moved to California. There in 1927 she wed her teenage sweetheart Chuck McGrew, though the marriage was short-lived and the couple divorced in 1929. The kid from Kansas, now renamed Jean Harlow, took a series of bit-parts in movies to help pay the rent, her career being managed – or rather mismanaged – by Bello and her mother, who adopted the soubriquet 'Mama Jean'. Between them, they would cream off most of the money the actress ever made.

Jean Harlow and her manipulative mother in 1934.

Jean appeared in a Laurel and Hardy film and a kindly Stan Laurel recommended her to agent Arthur Landau, who was to become a lifelong friend. Her breakthrough came when Howard Hughes signed her up and made her a star in the 1930 movie *Hell's Angels*. Two years later, after a string of minor movies, she switched to MGM and became a superstar in the 1932 hit *Red Dust*. Jean set a style of raw sensuality that broke the mould of previous, simpering leading ladies. She was the first Hollywood actress to appear regularly without a bra. Neither did she tend to wear any underwear, although she carefully died her pubic hair platinum to match the hair on her head. She also had a wily habit of rubbing ice on her nipples to make them stand out.

Studio boss Louis B. Mayer lauded her as representing 'normal sex, real sex, beautiful sex – the pure sex that is common to the people of America'. However, although her fans never knew it until after her death, 'normal sex' was not one of the things Jean Harlow was about to enjoy.

That same year, the 21-year-old star married a 40-year-old MGM film producer named Paul Bern, a quiet, sensitive man who, unlike her stepfather, had provided a fund of good advice for the furtherance of Jean's career. Bern took his bride home for a wedding night that proved to be a disaster. Two months later, on the night of 4 September 1932, he was dead, shot with a bullet through the head from his own .38 pistol. The butler discovered the naked body sprawled beneath a full-length mirror. It was drenched in his wife's favourite perfume, Mitsouko.

Bern left a suicide note: 'Dearest Dear, Unfortunately this is the only way to make good the frightful wrong I have done you and to wipe out my abject humiliation. I love you – Paul.' He added a mysterious postscript: 'You understand that last night was only a comedy.' Three days later another suicide was discovered. The body of Dorothy Milette, who had claimed to be Bern's common-law wife before Jean had married him, was found in the Sacramento River.

The ensuing scandal caused worldwide banner headlines but, despite the press speculation, Jean Harlow steadfastly refused to explain the meaning of Bern's note and the events that had led to his suicide. It took the actress's own untimely death five years later to bring the full story out in the open. According to her agent Arthur Landau, Jean had received a terrible shock on her wedding night when she discovered that her new husband was extraordinarily under-endowed and was probably impotent. She may have laughed at his sexual inadequacy or he may have been ashamed of his own attempts at lovemaking but the result was a beating for Jean.

The following morning, Jean telephoned Landau and asked him for help. He drove to Bern's house, found the producer sleeping naked on the floor and removed Jean to his own home. There she revealed that her husband had beaten her with a cane until it broke and had then hit her and bitten her on her legs and thighs. The fury of the attack sickened Landau but, after treatment by a doctor, Jean begged to be returned to the marital home. There the beaming newlyweds posed for formal wedding photographs at their VIP reception the following day.

The beating she had received, however, resulted in liver damage from which Jean never fully recovered. Yet the couple continued to play out an elaborate charade in public until the fateful day when Bern, who had banked on the screen goddess being able to cure his sexual problems, finally acknowledged his failure. He had arrived in the marital bedroom that night in a contraption designed to make the most of his meagre assets. His wife was disgusted. The following day Paul Bern put a gun to his head.

Harlow's reaction was not the usual one of a grieving widow. She embarked on a prolonged sex-and-booze binge, first in Los Angeles and then in San Francisco, in the course of which she cut off her

Screen passion: Harlow in 1932 movies *Red-Headed Woman* with Chester Morris and *Red Dust* with Clark Gable.

famous platinum blonde tresses. When she returned to Hollywood, Louis B. Mayer, who had suffered the impossible task of explaining away Bern's suicide note, ordered the studio wigmaker to repair the damage to his superstar's crowning asset. Mayer's patience finally ran out when Jean eloped in 1933 to marry her third husband, 38-year-old film cameraman Harold Rosson. The studio suspended her for a month; the marriage lasted eight.

Jean's next serious romance was with actor William Powell, probably the one true love of her life. She was still only 23 at the time they fell in love; he was 43, suave and sophisticated. On the third anniversary of their romance, he gave her a cake with the inscription: 'To my three-year-old from her Daddy.'

Harlow and husband Paul Bern.

Dearest dear,

Unfortunately this is the only way to make good the frightful wrong I have done you and to wipe out my abject humiliation. I love you.

Paul

You understand that last night was only a comedy

Paul Bern's suicide note and Harlow with Louis B. Mayer who helped in the cover-up.

Jean Harlow is helped from her car to attend the funeral of her husband Paul Bern.

Harlow wed cameraman Harold Rosson but the marriage was not a roaring success.

A twenty-year age difference, but actor William Powell was the one true love of her life.

Jean Harlow, the first real sex goddess of the 'talkies' cinema, died at the age of just 26.

Their genuine love never resulted in marriage. In 1937 Jean fell seriously ill with a bladder infection (and other complications), which poisoned her system; possibly because her mother, being a Christian Scientist, refused to call a doctor until it was too late. It may have been that Jean herself had refused hospital treatment or surgery. Jean Harlow died on 7 June at the age of 26. At the funeral, Nelson Eddy sang *Ah! Sweet Mystery of Life*. She was buried with a single gardenia in her hand and a card from William Powell that read, 'Good night, my dearest darling'.

CHAPTER FOUR

Errol Flynn

The sexual exploits of hell-raiser Errol Flynn began early. He lost his virginity at the age of 12 with a woman working for his family, whom he ungallantly described as 'plump blonde, not attractive but available'. At 17, he was kicked out of school 'after being caught with the daughter of a laundress'. His libido thereafter was unflagging. He changed partners like other people changed sheets, according to an ex-wife. Wholly lacking in modesty, he described himself as 'a walking phallic symbol' and boasted that he had spent between 12,000 and 14,000 nights in lovemaking.

The heart-throb intent on outraging the moral standards of the age was born in Tasmania on 20 June 1909, the son of well-heeled Anglo-Irish parents. He was sent to a private school in London and then to Sydney, where he was expelled for his tryst with the washerwoman's

daughter. From there, he began travelling the South Seas, taking jobs on ships and on docksides. While in New Guinea in the early 1930s, he was spotted by film producer Charles Chauvel who cast him as Fletcher Christian in a semi-documentary version of *Mutiny on the Bounty*. On the strength of that, Flynn returned to England to take acting jobs before moving to the US. On the transatlantic voyage, he met and eventually married Lili Damita, an actress five years his senior whose contacts proved valuable when they arrived in Los Angeles. Warner Bros were casting a big-budget movie, *Captain Blood*, and wanted either Robert Donat or Leslie Howard to play the lead. Flynn was put forward for a screen test and immediately offered a contract. The film was a huge hit and a new star was born. Flynn spent the next two decades playing the archetypal swashbuckler in a string of successful adventure films.

Off-screen, Flynn strode through Hollywood leaving a trail of sex scandals and press cuttings reporting his hell-raising, boozing, fighting and womanizing. His appeal to beautiful women was legendary, his prowess in bed unquestioned. When he acquired fame and fortune, he bought a yacht called *Sirocco*, which he nicknamed *Cirrhosis by the Sea*, and moved to a mansion in the Hollywood Hills that he equipped with an 'Orgy Room'. 'He would change women as quickly as his valet could change the sheets,' said his second wife, actress and socialite Nora Eddington, whom he wed a year after his 1942 divorce from the disillusioned Lili Damita.

The actor claimed 'I like my whiskey old and my women young', and these tastes caught up with him in 1942 when two girls, whom he nicknamed 'Jailbait' and 'San Quentin quail', laid complaints against him with the Los Angeles police. One said he had ravished her by land, the other claimed it was by sea, on his yacht. He went into court in 1943 charged with statutory rape, the Californian legal term for sex with a minor.

The trial was a farce. Nightclub dancer Peggy 'La Rue' Satterlee appeared in court in pigtails and bobbysocks, attempting to persuade the jury that she was 16 at the time of the alleged offence. She claimed she had been seduced on the schooner *Sirocco* after Flynn had removed all her clothes except her shoes and socks. However, Satterlee failed to convince the court that she was under 18 and Flynn, who admitted having seduced her, was acquitted.

A second girl, 17-year-old waitress Betty Hansen, told a strangely similar story. She alleged that Flynn had flirted with her at a tennis party and then followed her upstairs when she began to feel ill. He had laid her on a bed, taken off all her clothes except her shoes and socks and had then 'put his private parts in my private parts'. The courtroom erupted in laughter. Again Flynn was acquitted,

Studio photos of the young Errol Flynn.

Flynn with first wife Lili Damita, who provided contacts to the Hollywood hierarchy.

Flynn's second wife Nora Eddington in 1943 and third wife Patrice Wymore in 1950.

after the prosecution admitted that a charge against Satterlee of oral intercourse and one against Hansen of illegal abortion had both been dropped so that they could testify against the actor.

Flynn had, however, broken Hollywood's golden rule: Thou shalt not get caught. After the court case, he said: 'I was attacked as a sex criminal. I knew I could never escape this brand, that I would always be associated in the public mind with an internationally-followed rape case.' He was right. Although he enjoyed a brief period of notoriety among his drinking buddies, he was not offered another film role for a full year.

Marriage could not change him. After his second ended in divorce, he wed American stage and television actress Patrice Wymore in Monaco in 1950. Just before the

Flynn's charm and physique won women galore.

ceremony, Flynn was detained for an alleged assault on a 17-year-old girl. Accused and accuser came face-to-face in a police station and Flynn protested: 'As soon as I saw her hairy legs I knew I was innocent. Drunk, sober, drugged or partly insane, these were not the legs Flynn would have next to his.' The charge was dropped.

By now, Flynn was living one long drunken binge as he bar-hopped from Hollywood to London to his estate in Jamaica. He drank vodka as if it were water and was also addicted to morphine. He died, principally of a heart attack, in October 1959 at the age of 50, leaving his loyal widow Patrice a 2,000-acre coconut plantation. The actor also left a teenaged girlfriend…

With Flynn when he died was 17-year-old Beverly Aadland, who had accompanied him to Vancouver, Canada, where he was arranging the lease of his yacht, supposedly so that he could fund a further divorce and wed his teen lover. The actor had enjoyed a two-year affair with the girl, having seduced her at the age of 15, although with her parents' knowledge and with the excuse that he had been led to believe she was 18. He arranged for the budding actress to co-star with him in *Cuban Rebel Girls*, a 1959 B-movie unmemorable apart from being Flynn's last. Beverly's mother, Florence, later wrote a book, *The Big Love*, in which she tried to excuse the under-age romance. Beverly herself, although publicity-shy, also confirmed the affair, which had been extremely risky for the aged lothario having already suffered the 1943 statutory rape allegations by two under-age girls. In a 1988 article for *People* magazine, Beverly wrote: 'I was scared. He was just too strong for me. I cried.

Flynn's yacht Sirocco was nicknamed Cirrhosis by the Sea.

At one point he tore my dress. Then he carried me off to another room, and I was still carrying on. What was going through my head was, what was I going to tell my mother?' Her relationship with Flynn was the subject of the 2013 movie *The Last of Robin Hood*, in which Flynn was played by Kevin Kline and Aadland by Dakota Fanning.

The revelation of his affair with Beverly Aadland was not the only battering that Flynn's image took after his death. Michael Freedland, author of the unflattering biography *Errol Flynn*, alleged that one of the star's female conquests told her friends that he was poorly endowed. Another claimed that he sprinkled cocaine on his private parts to prolong lovemaking. Freedland also said that Flynn was hooked on hard drugs. Author Charles Higham claimed in his book *Errol Flynn: The Untold Story* that the star had been a Nazi spy during the Second World War. Demolishing the image of patriotic heroism surrounding the actor, Higham alleged that Flynn's loyalty to neutral Ireland led him to forge top-level Nazi contacts in the US and Mexico. He also claimed that Flynn was virulently anti-Semitic, referring to studio boss Jack Warner as 'that Jewish bastard'.

The author also accused Flynn of encouraging his reputation as a great womanizer because he was often a failure in bed. Worse, Higham claimed that Flynn was bisexual and had several homosexual affairs, including one with fellow screen idol Tyrone Power. In his biography of Flynn, he alleged that the pair became lovers during a three-week Mexican holiday in 1948. Flynn went on to have other male lovers, said Higham, who claimed that his information came from the star's former secretary, Dorothy Nolan. Higham wrote of Flynn and Power: 'Here were the two greatest Hollywood stars of their times, emblems of virility and masculinity, in bed together.' Flynn, he added, was terrified that his homosexuality might be discovered because it would have meant the end of his Hollywood career.

Higham's allegations were given credence by another book, *The Secret Life of Tyrone Power* by Hector Arce, who claimed the screen hero had in his early, struggling days accepted propositions from wealthy men in return for a meal. The writer said Power, who died in 1950, tried to disguise his homosexuality by embarking on a string of widely-publicized affairs with, among others, Judy Garland, Mai Zetterling, Anita Ekberg and Lana Turner. However, according to Arce, these liaisons were no more than a smokescreen for his homosexual activities.

Whatever the truth about Errol Flynn's proclivities, there is no doubt that the hell-raiser's sexual shenanigans were rampant. Further revelations about them came quite by chance in 1978 when his Hollywood Hills mansion was put up for sale at $2 million. Developers surveying the property discovered that the sex palace had bedrooms fitted with two-way mirrors and microphones. He and guests at his bawdy parties would watch as other couples paired off for sex romps. As a real estate agent said at the time: 'The orgies that went on there would make Hollywood today look like a Sunday school.'

There is one further disputed legacy of the old hell-raiser: the expression 'in like Flynn' is said to have been coined to refer to the ease with which he seduced women. Though its origin is disputed, Flynn was fond of the expression and wanted to call his autobiography *In Like Me*. The publisher insisted on a more tasteful title, *My Wicked, Wicked Ways*.

Flynn's young accusers: Peggy Satterlee (left) and Betty Hansen in court with their lawyer.

Portraying themselves as under-age: dark-haired Peggy Satterlee and blonde Betty Hansen. Satterlee was also photographed on the actor's yacht.

Flynn with the last love of his life, Beverly Aadland, and together on the set of *Cuban Rebel Girls*.

Beverly Aadland being interviewed after Flynn's sudden death in 1959.

Flynn's macho image was dented when actor Tyrone Power was named as an ex-lover.

CHAPTER FIVE

Grace Kelly

Grace Kelly was Hollywood royalty. The queen of the silver screen captivated moviegoers with her classical beauty and demure image. Eventually she really did become royalty, marrying her Prince Charming to become Princess Grace of Monaco and residing in a magnificent palace. It sounded like a fairytale in which everyone lives happily ever after, except that her story did not turn out like that and the image of the strait-laced virginal blonde was a fabricated myth.

The truth was that the Hollywood ice queen was a passionate playmate whose need for affection led her to bed some of the biggest stars in the movie business, among them Clark Gable, Gary Cooper, Tony Curtis, David Niven, Marlon Brando, Bing Crosby and Frank Sinatra. Yet her love life remained secret during her phenomenal movie career and, largely, throughout her apparently perfect royal partnership. The full extent of her scandalous sexual exploits was revealed only after her tragic death in 1982 in a series of devastating biographies that utterly tarnished the regal image of poor Princess Grace.

Grace Patricia Kelly was born on 12 November 1929 to a wealthy Philadelphia couple. The third of four children, she didn't have the best role model when it came to men, her philandering businessman father Jack Kelly enjoying affairs behind his wife's back. According to family friends, Jack, a 6ft 2in Olympic rower and self-made construction millionaire, favoured his elder daughter Peggy and it was Grace's obsession with gaining his approval that may later have powered a string of torrid affairs with unsuitable older

men in a desperate search for a father figure.

As a child, Grace had been no beauty. She wore glasses, was overweight and became insecure about having a small bust. However, acting in school plays helped her confidence and by her teenage years the boys at her private school began to take notice. As her socialite mother Margaret later boasted: 'Men began proposing to Grace when she was barely 15.' After graduating, Grace attended

Wealthy Philadelphia couple Jack and Margaret Kelly with their four children. Grace is top left.

the American Academy of Dramatic Arts in New York, where she fell for her Jewish acting teacher, 30-year-old Don Richardson. He was married but seeking a divorce, so the affair was kept secret until Grace's parents insisted on meeting the mysterious boyfriend. When she took her lover to Philadelphia, however, her father offended the guest with his anti-Semitic outbursts and her mother, having rifled through his suitcase, discovered his marital status and they ordered him from the house. 'The fact that I could fall in love with a Jew was beyond them,' Kelly said in a letter to a friend.

Kelly assured her parents that the affair was ended, but she continued seeing her lover in secret. Her biographer Wendy Leigh claimed in her 2007 book *True Grace* that while still in a relationship with Richardson, the actress also became involved with the notorious playboy Aly Khan. She also alleged that in 1949 Grace had a brief fling with the Shah of Iran who was visiting the US at the time. Don Richardson talked about his liaison with Kelly to another of her biographers, Robert Lacey, who, in his 1994 book titled simply *Grace*, relates how the teacher invited his new student to his apartment for coffee. He left her in the living room and when he came back she was naked. She was proud of her body, Richardson recalled, and not the least bit reluctant to show it off, but he added: 'She had become a career carnivore. She was rapacious about getting famous and being important. She'd already talked to me about some of the men she'd been dating, how they helped her to make social contacts and were teaching her things she needed to know.'

Grace: from fresh-faced innocence to sophisticated beauty.

By now Grace had grown into a blonde, blue-eyed beauty with luminescent skin, long limbs and sensuous lips. She was offered her first acting role in a Broadway play and performed in more than sixty live television dramas before getting her first film offer. Her screen debut came at the age of 22 with a small part in the 1951 suspense drama *Fourteen Hours*, but her big breakthrough was in the following year when she won the role of Amy, the young Quaker bride, in *High Noon* opposite Gary Cooper. During the four-week shoot, she had affairs simultaneously with Cooper, who was twenty-eight years her senior and already in a relationship with actress Patricia Neal, and with director Fred Zinnemann, who was also married and more than twenty years older than her.

The next year, 1953, brought another major role and another major mixed-up romance. In the movie *Mogambo* she received the Golden Globe Award for Best Supporting Actress and an Oscar nomination in the same category. The prize she was really after, however, was her co-star Clark Gable, who was as great a womanizer as Grace was a man-eater. Actress Ava Gardner had warned Grace off Gable but she was undeterred, even though she knew that Gable himself had his sights set on seducing Ava. To confuse matters further, Ava was already in a fiery relationship with Frank Sinatra, who would later also become Grace's lover. When Gable eventually realized he had no chance with Ava, he turned his attention to Grace, although he ended their affair when filming neared completion

Affair… with *High Noon* co-star Gary Cooper.

Affair… with *Mogambo* co-star Clark Gable.

three months later. An unrequited Grace then laid siege to Gable, who was forced to move hotels to avoid her and post a guard outside his suite.

As seemed to be the case with Grace, another year brought another film and another tangled love affair. In 1954, during the filming of Alfred Hitchcock's *Dial M for Murder*, she fell for her co-star Ray Milland, who had been married, apparently happily, for thirty years. The couple was seen together so openly that Milland's wife Mal threw him out and Kelly was in danger of being branded a home-wrecker. To salvage her reputation, the actress demurely issued a public statement and Milland returned to his forgiving wife. The pithiest verdict on Grace Kelly's threat to Hollywood wives came from the widow of one of them. Skip Hathaway, the widow of Henry Hathaway who directed Kelly in *Fourteen Hours*, told author Robert Lacey: 'Grace Kelly was a conniving woman. She almost ruined my best friend Mal's marriage. Kelly fucked everything in sight. She was worse than any woman I'd ever known.' When asked just how many men Grace had seduced, she added: 'Everybody. Yes, she wore white gloves but she was no saint.'

Wendy Leigh's biography supports the picture of Kelly as a sex siren. She is alleged to have had a fling with David Niven while he was married. Likewise, she fell for Bing Crosby on their first meeting, while his wife Dixie was battling terminal cancer. Grace believed he was marriage material but the suave star, who was twenty-six years her senior, was also seeing actress Kathryn Grant, who eventually became the next Mrs Crosby. Her bid for Crosby's commitment was not helped by one incident when he is said to have walked in on Grace as she lay naked in bed with Marlon Brando. Frank Sinatra's affair with her is said to have lasted for years, with a secret love nest in the South of France. She was 'my dream girl', the singer confided to his valet. Other co-stars she dated included Cary Grant and William Holden. On the list of alleged lovers were also actor Tony Curtis, US tennis ace Sidney Wood, British producer Anthony Havelock-Allan and musician Richard Boccelli. 'Grace was basically a romantic,' said Leigh. 'She was attracted to high-energy, driven men. There was a string of them, from gangsters to princes and many in between.'

In *Princess Grace* published in 1994, celebrity biographer Sarah Bradford confirmed her subject's 'passionate love affairs' with William Holden, Clark Gable and Ray Milland, who was 'gaga over her'. However, she believes that it was Grace who 'dropped Ray like a hot potato' when his wife threatened divorce. The book also questions the widely-rumoured romance with Bing Crosby, claiming that it was Bing who allowed the word to be spread that he had enjoyed Grace's favours.

On screen, Grace Kelly's stature as an international superstar was underpinned by her role in the second film she made for Hitchcock in

Affair… with *Dial M for Murder* co-star Ray Milland, who 'was gaga over her'.

1954, *Rear Window* opposite James Stewart. That same year, she won the Best Actress Oscar for her role alongside Bing Crosby and William Holden in *The Country Girl*. She re-teamed with Hitchcock for *To Catch a Thief* with Cary Grant in 1955. The following year she was alongside Crosby and Frank Sinatra in the musical *High Society*. Though her movie career spanned only five years and eleven films, when she retired from acting at the age of 26, she had left an immense impression on Hollywood filmgoers and on many of its male stars.

She clearly cast a spell over Prince Rainier, who she met while in Cannes for the 1955 film festival. The head of the House of Grimaldi had been led to believe that Grace was a virginal, worthy choice to be his wife and the mother of his children and he proposed within days. Before their betrothal, Rainier supposedly asked David Niven which of his lovers had been best in bed. 'Grace, of course,' he replied before hastily recalling the name of a less youthful English singer and adding: 'Er, Gracie Fields.' Grace Kelly's mother didn't help things when, in a US article published on the eve of the royal marriage, she confirmed her daughter's affairs with a string of leading men including Cooper, Gable, Milland, Crosby and Holden.

Her decision to marry Prince Rainier was especially tough, for she had already been secretly engaged to Russian fashion designer Oleg Cassini. It was even rumoured that she had become pregnant by him but had undergone an abortion. Cassini, who made his name designing elegant outfits for both her and Jacqueline Kennedy, confirmed: 'We were in love. We were engaged to be married. That is the truth. No more, no less.' In 1955 Grace

Grace's affair with Ray Milland caused his wife Mal to throw him out of the house.

took Cassini to meet her parents. Her mother particularly disliked him. In yet another biography, author J. Randy Taraborrelli claimed that ditching Cassini in favour of Rainier was an attempt by Grace to gain the approval of her father, who had failed to congratulate her on any of her past accomplishments. In his 2003 book *Once Upon a Time: Behind the Fairy Tale of Princess Grace and Prince Rainier*, the screen goddess is quoted as saying: 'Do you realize if my mother hadn't been so difficult about Oleg Cassini, I probably would have married him?' Indeed, she grew to regret not choosing a marriage that would have allowed her to continue her Hollywood career. 'How many wonderful roles I might have played by now?' she lamented. 'How might my life have turned out?'

Nine months after what was termed 'the wedding of the century' watched by 30 million TV viewers, Grace gave birth to the first of their three children: Caroline in 1957, then Albert in 1958, to be followed by Stéphanie in 1965. Despite focusing on her new role as a royal leader and mother, the marriage was turning out to be a sham. According to Robert Lacey, the prince was 'a moody and sometimes tyrannical husband' and his wife felt like a prisoner in the pink-painted Grimaldi palace. Bowing to her husband's wishes to forgo further acting offers, her loneliness and boredom were soon replaced by severe

Grace dated co-stars Cary Grant (*To Catch a Thief*, 1955) and Bing Crosby (*High Society*, 1956).

depression. She did briefly accept Alfred Hitchcock's offer of the lead role in the 1964 thriller *Marnie* but pressure from the people of Monaco forced her to withdraw.

Her frustration led to Grace becoming, in Lacey's words, 'a libertine who continued to indulge her sensuality to the full', in the knowledge that her husband was also enjoying extra-marital flings. Having seemingly lost her need for a father figure, the princess instead entertained younger men who would make her feel young again despite her ballooning figure. Actress Rita Gam, an old friend and a bridesmaid at her wedding, said: 'Grace was used by some of these men. For them it was not so serious but for her it was. They did not suffer as desperately and as silently as she did.' Another of her bridesmaids had a less charitable view of the princess's passions. Model Carolyn Reybold had been so close to the star that Grace named her first child after her, but that friendship wasn't to last after she bedded Carolyn's wealthy husband, Malcolm. According to Wendy Leigh, Grace eventually confessed all, blaming it on her distress after her father was found to have cancer, but the betrayal left Carolyn a broken woman; her life spiralled out of control after her marriage collapsed and she ended up living in homeless shelters.

Grace's marriage to Prince Rainier of Monaco was dubbed 'the wedding of the century'.

The double life of Princess Grace came to a sad and sudden end on 13 September 1982 when her car crashed on a hairpin bend overlooking the Mediterranean near Monaco. With her was Princess Stéphanie, who suffered only minor injuries but her mother never regained consciousness. She survived for thirty-six hours and was still clinically alive when her husband agreed with doctors that they could switch off her life-support system. The likelihood was that the 52-year-old princess had suffered a stroke, causing her Rover to veer off down the mountainside, but that did not prevent the media having a field day with theories of assassination, murder and suicide. Thus, in death, as the presses rolled and the biographies hit the bookshops, the former movie queen again became the most talked-about Hollywood superstar of the age.

Royal waves and regal poses… but the 'fairytale' marriage soon ran into serious trouble.

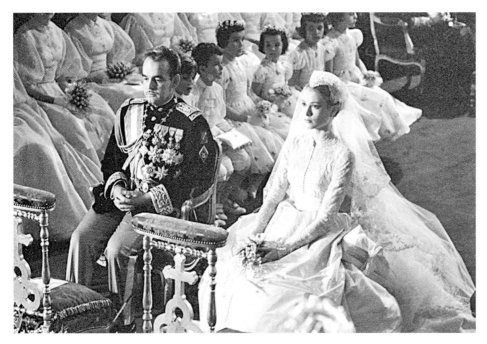

Changing face
of a princess:
sombre at her
wedding in
1956; pensive
in a family
portrait in
1966; smiling at
a Paris fashion
show in 1979.

The car in which Princess Grace crashed in 1982 on a road overlooking the Mediterranean...

...a similar vista to the one she and Cary Grant shared in their 1955 film *To Catch a Thief*.

CHAPTER SIX

Lana Turner

Jerry Giesler's home telephone number was known to most Hollywood stars. As California's most prestigious lawyer, he was the man they called at the slightest whiff of trouble, from traffic violations to small-print problems with a movie contract. However, the phone call he received at 10.00 pm on the night of 4 April 1958 was far more serious. The woman at the other end of the line was Lana Turner, one of the biggest names on the silver screen. Yet the assured, silky voice familiar to movie fans around the world sounded desperate. 'Something terrible has happened,' she told him.

Giesler sped to her Beverly Hills home to comfort and advise the actress – and possibly enhance the evidence for her. Certainly, when the local police chief arrived, he was certain

that he had worked out what had happened. Lana's boyfriend Johnny Stompanato was lying on the floor, stabbed to death with an 8in carving knife. The actress and her 14-year-old daughter Cheryl Crane were in the room, both distraught as Cheryl cried 'I didn't mean to kill him' and Lana begged the policeman: 'Please let me say that I did it.' The cop was having none of it.

Lana Turner was the original Hollywood 'sweater girl', an honorary title that had nothing to do with her knitting ability but everything to do with how studio bosses had capitalized on the evident charms of her ample breasts. Her film career had begun in 1937 when she was just 16 years old, newly-arrived in Los Angeles from her home in Wallace, Idaho. She established herself as a leading actress through the 1940s with movies such as *Johnny Eager*, *Ziegfeld Girl* and *The Postman Always Rings Twice*. These hits were followed by a string of flops, which could also have been the description of her four failed marriages at that stage (Artie Shaw, Steve Crane, Bob Topping and Lex Barker) and several love affairs (Howard Hughes, Tyrone Power, Fernando Lamas and Frank Sinatra).

However, in 1957 her muddled marital arrangements and shaky career seemed to have turned the corner. She was 37, living with her teenaged daughter from her second marriage, and she had a major hit on her hands. Her new movie *Peyton Place* brought her an Oscar nomination.

Then a fresh disaster walked into her life. As she was getting over the collapse of her latest marriage, to Lex Barker, she accepted a blind date with smooth-talking hoodlum Johnny Stompanato, an ex-US Marine, con-man and associate of known gangsters. It was the biggest mistake of her life.

Stompanato was the 'muscle' for gangster Mickey Cohen, himself an associate of the big-league mobster Bugsy Siegel. However, the cash he made from his modest income through theft and fencing stolen goods was never enough for his extravagant needs. One way he got around this was to attach himself to wealthy women prepared to bankroll him. In Hollywood slang, this made him a 'fee-male' (it was the woman who always paid the fees), but it did not deter Lana who, like his three previous wives, was at first captivated by his charm and good looks.

Stompanato wooed her by sending a succession of bouquets to the studio where she was filming *The Lady Takes a Flyer*. The flowers carried no message; only the name John Steele and a phone number. When Lana rang and spoke to her mysterious admirer, he told her that they had a mutual friend in fellow film star Ava Gardner. It was a lie but she never checked and foolishly gave him her phone number. 'This is how the blackest period of my life began,' she later mourned. 'What happened I can never forget, but why it happened I'll never really understand.'

Lana Turner, husband Steve Crane and baby Cheryl.

Lana with young Cheryl in the late 1940s.

Hollywood's original 'sweater girl' in more elegant studio pose.

Lana with Lee Philips in *Peyton Place*.

The unlikely pair became lovers, and the star allowed the crook to move into her mansion. There he bullied her, abused her, took her money and spent it on gambling. They fought interminably but Lana Turner appeared not to be able to live without him. Daughter Cheryl begged her mother to end the relationship, with Lana replying simply: 'I'm too afraid.' She had good reason to be.

Towards the end of 1957, Lana made one determined attempt to shake him off. She flew to Britain to make *Another Time, Another Place*, which involved romantic scenes with a rising young star called Sean Connery. Jealous Stompanato borrowed the air fare from Mickey Cohen and turned up in London to haunt her. When he was barred from the set, he arrived at her rented house and tried to smother her with a pillow. 'I'm not kidding around,' he threatened. 'I can take care of your mother and Cheryl too. Don't think I won't do it. I can have it done. No one will ever know where it came from.' The final straw came when he burst onto the film set carrying a gun and had to be restrained by the burly Connery, who deftly disarmed him. Lana rang the police and Stompanato was escorted onto a plane home.

With her lover more than 5,000 miles away, fickle Lana longed to be with him again. She stupidly wrote to him: 'To say how much you are and have been missed is almost impossible. I dare not, even to myself, admit how much.' They had a reunion in Acapulco, Mexico, and she presented him with a keepsake, a bracelet bearing the inscription in Spanish: 'My sweet love, remember a piece of my heart will be with you always – Lana.'

Yet little in the violent relationship had changed. On the fateful night in April 1958, Stompanato had a screaming row with his mistress. He threatened to scar her at the very least. According to police evidence, Cheryl was listening outside the door. She heard Stompanato say: 'I'll get you if it takes a day, a week, a month or a year. If I can't do it myself, I'll get someone who will. That's my business.' Cheryl entered the room carrying a long-bladed kitchen knife, thrust it into his torso and killed him.

Right: Lana dining out with her violent lover Johnny Stompanato, a conman and hoodlum who bullied and abused her.

Below: A Los Angeles cop examines the body of Stompanato, stabbed to death in Lana's home.

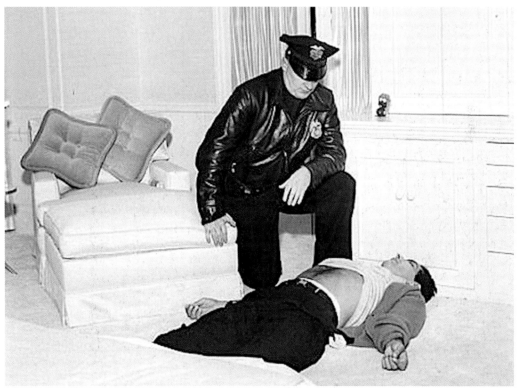

Lana Turner's 14-year-old daughter Cheryl Crane is taken into custody suspected of murder.

The ensuing inquest was sensational. Televised live, it got audience figures higher even than *Peyton Place* and the evidence proved racier than any movie. Even the couple's love letters were produced as every detail of the sordid affair was aired. Lana Turner gave the performance of her life in the witness box. Under astute questioning from lawyer Jerry Giesler, she quoted the thug's threats to her: 'I'll mutilate you. I will hurt you so you'll be so repulsive that you'll have to hide forever.' On the night of the stabbing, he had ordered her: 'When I say hop, you hop. When I say jump, you jump.'

Cheryl was allowed to give her evidence in writing. Her statement read:

> They had an argument and he was threatening mother. He said he would kill her and hurt daddy, grandma and me. He said he had ways of doing it. My mother was very frightened. I went down to the kitchen and got the knife. I took it up to the room in case he hurt mother. I rushed into the room and stuck him with the knife. He screamed.

Lana's evidence completed the gory train of events:

> Mr Stompanato stumbled forward, turned around and fell on his back. He choked, his hands on his throat. I ran to him and lifted up his sweater. It was the blood … he made a horrible noise in his throat. I tried to breathe air into his semi-open lips, my mouth against his. He was dying.

The jury speedily returned a verdict of justifiable homicide, effectively acquitting Cheryl of blame for the killing. A friend of Stompanato leaped up in the public gallery and shouted: 'It's lies, all lies. The girl was in love with him as well. He was killed because of jealousy between mother and daughter.' Some evidence for that outlandish claim was provided later by Cheryl herself. In her 1988 autobiography, *Detour: A Hollywood Story*, she alleged that Stompanato had been sexually abusing her, as had one of her mother's previous husbands.

Cheryl Crane at the inquest with her mother and lawyer Jerry Giesler (centre).

Lana gives evidence at the inquest, which returned a verdict of 'justifiable homicide'.

Then, in 2017, further claims about the supposed under-aged affair were published, with an entirely new version of the events on the night of the killing. Veteran Hollywood biographer Darwin Porter said the actress had confessed to close friends that she was really the killer. In his book, *Lana Turner: Hearts and Diamonds Take All*, Porter said that lawyer Jerry Giesler, who Turner rang before calling the police, rearranged the crime scene with the help of a well-known Hollywood private detective, Fred Otash. Before his death in 1992, Otash allegedly admitted: 'I received a call from Mr Giesler telling me, "Get right over here. Stompanato's on Lana's bed, which looks like a hog was butchered." From what I gathered, Lana had walked in on Johnny in bed with Cheryl. She went for the knife and plunged it into his stomach.' Otash admitted being 'a naughty boy' by wiping Lana's fingerprints off the murder weapon.

It is certainly true that Giesler urged his client to let her daughter take the blame because, as a minor, she would not face a full trial. Stories were rehearsed and Cheryl was crying that she 'didn't mean to kill him' when police chief Clinton Anderson arrived.

The two wildly conflicting versions of the killing are as different as the lives followed by the two suspects, mother and daughter. Poor Cheryl's life remained in turmoil after her release from juvenile detention. She was made a ward of the court and, at her own request, placed in the custody of Turner's mother. She ran away from home and from a state boarding school and pursued a life of drinking and pill-taking before becoming a real estate broker.

As for her mother, the *Los Angeles Times* summed up the public sentiment towards Turner, accusing her of showing 'the lack of almost any reference to moral sensitivity in the presence of a child.' The scandal had no ill effects on her career, however. *Peyton Place* played to packed houses and she earned an incredible $2 million from her next film, *Imitation of Life*. In the 1980s she took on a recurring guest role in the television soap opera *Falcon Crest*. However, she never got her Oscar. The dramas on the screen never lived up to her most amazing real-life romance and tragedy. When she died in 1995, aged 74, she had been married seven times, yet questions about her most scandalous love affair had still not been laid to rest.

Abuse claims: Cheryl Crane's 1988 autobiography.

Lana Turner returned to the screen in the 1980s in the TV series *Falcon Crest*.

CHAPTER SEVEN

Marilyn Monroe

The last day that the world's most famous female film star appeared on set was also her thirty-sixth birthday. After a day's shooting at the Fox studios on 1 June 1962, a cake was produced for Marilyn Monroe as she happily celebrated the event. Afterwards, however, she called in sick, repeating excuses for her non-appearances that had infuriated director George Cukor. Marilyn was fired and the movie abandoned. Its title was *Something's Got to Give* … and something did.

Two months later, just before dawn on Sunday, 5 August 1962, Monroe's naked body was discovered sprawled across her bed at her Los Angeles home. The greatest sex goddess of all had millions of fans around the world, many powerful friends and countless lovers, yet she died alone, and in death, as in life, her troubled personality was the subject of sensation and scandal.

The years that have passed since her death have not dimmed her legend. Instead it has been fanned by revelations of her amazing sexual exploits, outrageous behaviour and secret affairs with stars and politicians including, it is alleged, US President Jack Kennedy himself. It has been revealed that she was abused as a child, was promiscuous in her teens, performed sexual favours for studio tycoons and ended up seeking gratification with her personal staff.

Ironically, the sex goddess lusted after by millions often failed to find satisfaction in sex. In her frenzied affairs she was seeking a joy and a release that seldom came to her. She once said she was hooked on sex like an alcoholic is hooked on liquor, and there were plenty of opportunities to indulge her craving. 'My body turns people on like an electric light,' she said. Those who succumbed included a handsome masseur who she hired so that she could seduce him during their afternoon sessions. Other days she would invite her chauffeur to her room and lock the door for several hours. She supposedly told one of her lovers, young screenwriter Hans Lembourne:

> I don't know whether I'm good or bad in bed. I can't sustain loving relationships. I drink, I lie. I often want to die, though I'm deadly scared of death. I believe in marriage and faithfulness, yet I go to bed with others when I'm married. God help me, what a mess.

If the life of the girl the world came to know as Marilyn Monroe did turn out to be a mess, it had a lot to do with her childhood. Born Norma Jeane Mortensen on 1 June 1926, she never knew with certainty who her father was. He may have been Edward Mortensen, a Danish baker later killed in a motorcycle accident. Or he could have been Charles Stanley Gifford, a co-worker of Norma Jeane's mother, Gladys, in a Los Angeles film-cutting studio. The baby was in desperate need of maternal care but Gladys Monroe Baker Mortensen was emotionally disturbed and was eventually removed to an asylum. Norma Jeane was to spend her tenderest years in orphanages and with a succession of foster parents. It is believed that she was sexually abused while in one of the children's homes and that, at

Norma Jeane at the age of 3 with her emotionally-disturbed mother Gladys.

Norma Jeane, the tender teenager.

Marriage in 1942 to Jim Dougherty.

the age of 15, she was seduced by one of her foster fathers.

In 1942, shortly after her sixteenth birthday, Norma Jeane wed 21-year-old factory hand Jim Dougherty. The life of a working-class housewife soon bored her, and escape from dull routine came when her husband enlisted in the wartime merchant navy. When he was shipped to the Pacific, his pretty young wife killed time in bars and soon discovered that she could have more fun by going to men's hotel rooms with them. Years later, telling her maid Lena Pepitone of those escapades, she said: 'I let my husband do whatever he wanted with me even though I didn't really love him. So what was the difference?' Although the couple did not divorce until 1946, the marriage was well and truly over, with Jim overseas and Norma Jeane working in a Los Angeles munitions factory. There she was spotted by a visiting photographer commissioned by the US Air Force to take morale-boosting pictures of female workers. None was used but in 1945 she was encouraged to sign with a model agency. Her real target, however, was movieland.

Hollywood in the 1940s was, in her own words, 'an overcrowded brothel' and, as a model, she began getting invitations to many celebrity parties. A natural brunette, she had by now decided that gentlemen prefer blondes, but went further than her famous bleached hairstyle by also peroxiding her pubic hair, a painful process but essential with her habit of wearing sheer white dresses and no underwear. In her struggle for a toehold on the ladder to stardom, she admitted later that she would have slept with almost anybody, as long as they were 'nice'. She told Lena: 'If I made them happy, why not? It didn't hurt. I like to see men smile.' Among faces she had put a smile on, it was later claimed, was Twentieth Century Fox founder Joe Schenck, who was aged 70 and asked only that she sat with him in the nude while he fondled her breasts and talked about the good old days. Schenck introduced her to Columbia boss Harry Cohn who, she said, simply told her to get into bed. He was succeeded by comedian Milton Berle, who claimed: 'She wasn't out to please me because I might be able to help her but because she liked me.'

It was as a gangster's moll in the 1950 film *The Asphalt Jungle* that the budding star made her name – by this time changed to Marilyn Monroe – although still typecast in the 'dumb blonde' category. Producer Billy Wilder said: 'She has breasts like granite and a brain like cheese.' In fact, Marilyn was far from dumb but realized the value of maintaining that fiction. Her hero was the mathematician Albert Einstein and she later displayed a large framed photograph of him inscribed: 'To Marilyn, with love and thanks.'

The most loyal and devoted of all the men in Marilyn's life was her next husband, baseball star Joe DiMaggio. However, Joe hated her sex goddess image, believing that the only place she should be sexy was at home with him. He would do nothing to help her career, refusing to pose for publicity shots with her and never accompanying her to showbiz parties. They wed in 1954 and parted after nine months. 'What good is being a sex symbol if it drives your man away?' she said bitterly.

Dougherty enlisted in the merchant navy.

Even before marrying DiMaggio, she had been carrying a torch for her next husband, playwright Arthur Miller. When they wed in 1956, she felt that she had proved an important point. She was not just a dumb blonde. She was the wife of an intellectual. 'I've never loved anyone as much as I love Arthur,' she said. Her happiness was short-lived. She longed for a child by Miller and soon became pregnant, but she had a miscarriage after the sixth week. When her next pregnancy ended the same way, she was beside herself with grief, sobbing: 'I can never have kids again.'

Miller was soon spending little time with his beautiful wife. He shut himself away in his study, working all day and late into the evening while Marilyn pleaded for company before going to bed alone. As the couple drifted further apart, she turned to champagne, pills and a string of affairs with all sorts of lovers, from fellow actors to politicians and even to a plumber she had called to fix a leak.

Marilyn fell for French star Yves Montand as soon as she met him, and she was delighted to have him as her co-star in the 1960 musical comedy *Let's Make Love*. A brief affair flourished during filming, while Arthur Miller was away in Ireland and Montand's wife Simone Signoret was back in Paris. Marilyn hoped their affair would lead to marriage but, once filming was over, Montand thanked her for a 'nice time' and flew straight back to his wife. Marilyn was

Norma Jeane worked in a munitions factory.

left sobbing among the flowers and unopened champagne bottles in a hotel room she had booked for a romantic farewell.

She hoped that a friendship with Frank Sinatra would lead to a permanent relationship, but he insisted she keep out of sight when she was staying at his place. He was having affairs with other women and did not want any publicity. One evening, drunk on champagne and tired of waiting for him, she wandered nude into the room where he and some friends were playing poker. Furious, he hissed: 'Get your fat ass upstairs!' Marilyn was heartbroken when she heard that he was dating leggy dancer Juliet Prowse.

The end of her marriage to Miller came during filming of the 1961 drama *The Misfits*, which he wrote. Her blazing rows with him on set and her chaotic timekeeping were partly blamed for the death of her co-star, Clark Gable, who suffered a heart attack a day after filming ended. With this on her conscience and her marriage in ruins, she turned back to Joe DiMaggio for consolation. When he wasn't around, it was booze, pills and a succession of companions, among whom one liaison could have embroiled both of them in the scandal of the century. For Marilyn's sensational sexuality and her craving for love took her to the very top: to President John F. Kennedy.

As has since been revealed, most of Kennedy's 'affairs' were short-term, most lasting only an hour or so. Others were of greater importance to him and of the gravest worry to his secret service protectors. Among these was his love affair with the most feted beauty in the world. Kennedy used to pinch and squeeze her and tell her dirty jokes. He was fond of putting his hand up her skirt at the dinner table. One night he kept going until he discovered she wasn't wearing panties and, according to Marilyn, took his hand away fast. 'He hadn't counted on going that far,' she said. Kennedy had been introduced to Marilyn by his brother-in-law, actor Peter Lawford, who was married to Jack's sister Pat. Lawford had a Los Angeles beachfront home which was used as a Californian base both by Jack and his brother Robert, the US Attorney General. Both of them, it is now believed, had affairs with Marilyn.

The actress was desperately unstable at this time and luring her into these clandestine affairs did nothing to improve her mental state. At the height of her affair with Jack, Marilyn even travelled in disguise on the presidential aircraft Air Force One. She was there at his side at his forty-fifth birthday party in Madison Square Gardens on 19 May 1962 (ten days before the actual date) when she sang a shaky *Happy Birthday, Mr. President*. After that event, however, the Kennedys tried to distance themselves from her and her calls to the White House were unanswered.

Marilyn's health deteriorated and she relied increasingly on drink and drugs. As an indication of her state of mind, her maid Lena Pepitone later described her shock when she was interviewed for the job, with the actress totally naked and 'looking like a deluxe prostitute after a busy night in a plush brothel.' In her book *Marilyn Monroe Confidential*, Lena wrote: 'Her blonde hair looked unwashed and was a mess. I was astonished by the way she smelled. She needed a bath, badly. Without make-up, she was pale and tired-looking. Her celebrated figure seemed more overweight than voluptuous.' In the last year of her life, the sex goddess was noticing the signs of age. She complained that her breasts were getting flabby and she worried about stretch marks on her bust and bottom. 'I can't act,' she told Lena. 'When my face and body go, I'll be finished.'

When making her final movie, *Something's Got to Give*, she was taking more pills than ever. Complaining that she was suffering from bronchitis, she often did not arrive on the set until the afternoon, if at all. Finally, she was fired, her co-star Dean Martin quit and the film was abandoned. The shame of her career failure sent her into deeper depression. When, on 5 August 1962, her lifeless body was discovered at her newly-acquired home on Fifth Helena Drive in Brentwood, telltale empty pill bottles were on the bedside table. The conclusion was obvious: Marilyn had committed suicide. The inquest verdict went unquestioned for some months, but when at last doubts were raised, the resultant scandal threatened to be bigger than anything the actress had created in her lifetime. For the question

Norma Jeane in 1946, the year she changed her name.

To Marilyn, beauty contests were a step to stardom.

Sexual favours: Twentieth Century Fox's Joseph Schenk (left) and Columbia's Harry Cohn.

more and more people began to ask was: Who killed Marilyn Monroe? Did she die by her own hand – by accident or suicide – or was she murdered? When her body was found, she had been clutching a telephone. Who had she been trying to contact?

Rumours swept Hollywood about her affairs with Jack Kennedy and his brother Robert. It was suggested that Marilyn was planning to reveal the truth about both relationships. She felt that the Kennedys had used her and then abandoned her, and she was out for revenge. The only thing that could have stopped her revelations would have been a phone call from or a meeting with Robert Kennedy, who was in California at the time. It seems certain that Marilyn had tried to contact him at the Justice Department in Washington several times in the weeks before her death but her 'nuisance' calls had not been put through.

Several investigative writers advanced the theory that Marilyn had been murdered by secret service agents to protect the White House from scandal. Ex-husband Joe DiMaggio was one of those convinced that the Kennedys had her killed. Although he never spoke out in public, he sanctioned a posthumous memoir in which he claimed Marilyn knew too much about the Mafia links that had helped Jack Kennedy get elected and that had continued throughout his presidency.

A bizarre twist to this theory was revealed in a book, *Mafia Kingpin*, co-authored by reformed criminal Ronald 'Sonny' Gibson, who said that while working for the mob, he had learned of a deal between the Mafia and FBI chief J. Edgar Hoover. Gibson claimed that Hoover had been so concerned about Marilyn's affair with the president that he had agreed to turn a blind eye to her murder. The Mafia, who needed to repay old favours done for them by the FBI, sent out-of-town professional hitmen to kill her.

Right: Comic lover? Milton Berle.

Below: The world loved her voluptuous curves but Marilyn worried about her figure. In 1955 the 29-year-old took up weightlifting as part of her fitness regime.

The budding star made her name, by now changed to Marilyn Monroe, in the 1950 film *The Asphalt Jungle* in which she appeared as a gangster's moll opposite Sterling Hayden (right).

Marilyn's 1954 marriage to baseball star Joe DiMaggio lasted just nine months.

Above left and right: Joe DiMaggio was the most devoted man in Marilyn's life, but he hated her sex goddess image.

Right: Even before marrying DiMaggio, Marilyn had been carrying a torch for her next husband, Arthur Miller. The 1956 marriage of the sex goddess and the intellectual playwright stunned Hollywood.

Marilyn appeared devoted to Miller, until falling for French star Yves Montand (bottom left).

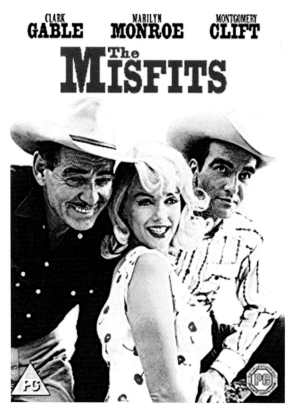

CLARK GABLE · MARILYN MONROE · MONTGOMERY CLIFT

The MISFITS

Monroe's marriage to Miller ended during filming of the appropriately titled *The Misfits*, which he wrote. Their on-set rows and her chaotic timekeeping were partly blamed for Clark Gable's fatal heart attack.

Marilyn with Robert and Jack Kennedy, both of whom were said to have been her lovers.

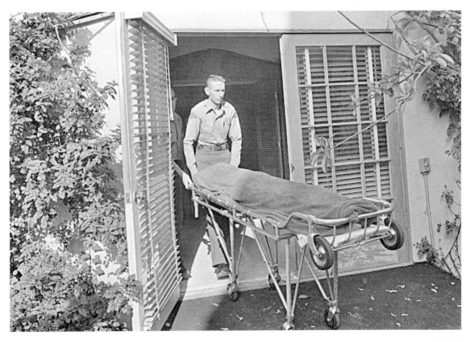

Marilyn's body is removed from her bedroom, where she was found on 5 August 1962.

A classic image of Marilyn Monroe, who was arguably the greatest screen sex goddess of all time. She had millions of admirers around the globe and had entertained dozens of lovers. Yet she died alone of an overdose of pills.

On the night she died, Marilyn was due to have attended a dinner at the home of Peter Lawford and his wife Pat. The actress had met Robert Kennedy at the house on several occasions and she may have hoped that he was planning to turn up. He never did. Nor did Marilyn, who at about 8.00 pm received a phone call from Peter Lawford asking if she was on her way. According to Lawford's testimony, she said she felt too tired. She told him: 'Say goodbye to Pat and say goodbye to the president ... and say goodbye to yourself, because you're such a nice guy.' Alarmed, Lawford rang back later. The line was engaged. It was not the first time that Marilyn Monroe was suspected of taking an overdose of pills, intentionally or otherwise, but previously there had been friends to revive her. On this occasion, no one came to her aid in time.

CHAPTER EIGHT

Jayne Mansfield

Most celebrities try to disguise their scandalous activities. The improbably pneumatic Jayne Mansfield gloried in them. There was nothing admirable about her weird lifestyle, however, and what had once seemed mere showbiz razzmatazz and glamorous eccentricity ended up as drug-fuelled madness, leading to the most horrific of deaths.

It must be admitted that Jayne Mansfield never reached the pinnacle of superstardom that would normally qualify her as a screen idol. Yet her face and body were as widely recognized around the world as those of many a genuinely talented actress. This top-heavy phenomenon, with a supposed genius-level IQ of 164 and with a bust measurement almost to match, was the most outrageous character in Hollywood in the late 1950s and 1960s, and she epitomized those scandalous decades as a star who never hid her sexual activities, whether good, bad or downright promiscuous.

Yet her life and acting career began in apparent sweetness and innocence. The future sex goddess was born Vera Jayne Palmer on 19 April 1933 in Bryn Mawr, Pennsylvania, to well-off parents of English and German ancestry. Her father, a successful lawyer practising in Phillipsburg, New Jersey, died of a heart attack when Jayne was 3 years old and her mother subsequently remarried and moved the family to Dallas, Texas. There, young Jayne took ballroom dancing lessons and studied Spanish and German. She also developed a talent for the piano and violin, holding concerts at home for friends and neighbours. She attended the city's university where she was a model student who took part in minor theatrical events.

In 1950, when only just 17, she married public relations agent Paul Mansfield, five years her senior, giving birth six months later to a daughter, Jayne Marie Mansfield. The family moved

At just 17, Jayne married Paul Mansfield, 22, and the curvaceous brunette became a regular beauty pageant contestant.

to Austin so that Jayne could study drama and, although she was rated as a future stage talent, she was best known for winning several less-than-prestigious beauty contests including Miss Photoflash, Miss Magnesium Lamp and Miss Fire Prevention Week. She also quietly embarked on some nude modelling.

Jayne was neither naïve nor poor; her academic qualifications were creditable and she had gained an inheritance from two aunts that was worth more than $1 million at today's value. When she and Paul Mansfield moved to Los Angeles in 1954 so that she could enrol in a theatre arts course at the University of California, it looked as if a stable future was at least secured. Then it all began to unravel.

Jayne had been given some low-budget movie roles by Warner Brothers before she finally seemed to have hit the big time in 1956 when 20th Century Fox, at that time embroiled in a feud with their leading lady Marilyn Monroe, signed her to a six-year contract. Believing they could mould her into a blonde bombshell successor to Monroe, they handed her over to director Frank Tashlin to put to best use her prime assets: pendulous breasts topping an unbelievable 40-18-36 figure. Tashlin accepted the task gleefully, stating: 'There's nothing more hysterical to me than big-breasted women, like walking leaning towers!' He packaged her in a comedy film *The Girl Can't Help It*. It was a success but virtually her only one.

Jayne undoubtedly had an acting talent but studio executives insisted on stereotyping her in dumb blonde roles. When she appeared in the favourably-reviewed 1957 comedy *Will Success Spoil Rock Hunter?*, critics unkindly termed her 'the poor man's Marilyn

Jayne's first movie was a rare success.

Monroe'. By the time she cavorted in the 1960 British gangster film *Too Hot to Handle*, her descent into low-budget productions and sleazy stage performances had begun.

Long before this sorry stage in her career, Jayne had decided that publicity could work where talent had failed. She ensured that her hair was always peroxide blonde, her lips scarlet, her flaunted bosom snowy white. Everything else was pink: her Cadillac, her clothes and her Sunset Strip home, complete with heart-shaped bed, bath and swimming pool. She became the ultimate attention-grabber, bursting into parties in honour of rival stars and flooding the press with items of gossip. Her most infamous publicity stunt had been in April 1957 when she used her breasts to steal the press limelight from actress Sophia Loren during a dinner party in the Italian star's honour. The brassy blonde plonked herself between Loren and her dinner companion, actor and dancer Clifton Webb, then leaned over the table to display her cleavage. Her ploy worked because the resulting photographs were published around the world, showing the disapproving Italian gazing at Mansfield's breasts as they threatened to spill over her low neckline. Loren said in a later interview that she was 'staring at her nipples because I am afraid they are about to come onto my plate.'

The publicity stunts may have occasionally worked out but Jayne's first marriage did not. Only days after a bitter divorce in 1958, she wed minor actor and bodybuilder Miklós 'Mickey' Hargitay, a former Mr Universe winner, with whom she had three children, one born after that five-year marriage also ended in divorce.

In the tempestuous years leading to that break-up, Jayne managed to fit in a series of well-publicized affairs, including one with the producer of her 1962 musical comedy *Panic Button*, Enrico Bomba, who Hargitay accused of sabotaging the marriage. The following year she was bedding singer Nelson Sardelli, who she said she planned to wed when her Mexican divorce from Hargitay was finalized in 1964. Instead, that same year she embarked on her third marriage, to film director Matt Cimber, which produced one child before that too ended in divorce in 1966.

By now a trademark blonde, Jayne Mansfield appeared opposite Tom Ewell in *The Girl Can't Help It.*

She immediately moved in with her lawyer Sam Brody, the couple finding time between drunken brawls to have one son, who was ultimately raised by ex-husband Cimber and his new wife. Between and during marriages, Jayne was said to have been intimately involved with a mixed bag of supposed admirers, from a Las Vegas entertainer to a Brazilian millionaire to the president of the United States, but separating fact from publicity fiction in her case is near impossible.

As Mansfield's career slid, so did Jayne herself, into a world of booze and drugs. What had once seemed harmless showbiz fun became a tawdry freak show, which ended horrifically on the night in 1967 when the car carrying her to a TV interview hit a truck, killing her instantly.

The razzmatazz that Jayne had encouraged throughout her life continued through to the funeral. Then the depth of her downward spiral towards dementia was finally revealed. Her youngest daughter, Jayne Marie, then aged 28, announced that she was writing a tell-all book. Although she never produced it, she and others close to the family branded the sex symbol a domestic monster living in a bizarre fantasy world of promiscuity, drugs, drink and even devil worship.

According to her daughter, Mansfield slept with Elvis Presley in the hope that he would sing for no fee in *The Girl Can't Help It*. The next morning, they agreed to toss a coin to decide. Jayne lost and Elvis gave her a pink motorcycle. Jayne was also said to have had an affair with Senator Robert Kennedy and to have attended beach house parties with John F. Kennedy and actor Peter Lawford. She would often tell her daughter: 'Mommy's off to a pyjama party.'

Jayne Marie complained that when she was a teenager, her mother made her dress like a little girl with her breasts

Her most infamous stunt: in 1957 Jayne used her breasts to steal the limelight from Sophia Loren.

Queen Elizabeth recognizes Jayne Mansfield's appeal at a London theatrical charity event in 1957. The Queen told her: 'I have just been to your country and they gave me a wonderful time.' Jayne answered: 'May I tell you, ma'am, that I think you are looking wonderful.' The Queen replied: 'Thank you, so are you.'

flattened. The reason, according to the daughter, was Jayne's fear that if she were seen with a teenage offspring it would make her seem old.

Jayne Marie's partner Greg Tyler, who supposedly enjoyed affairs with both mother and daughter, claimed that the star drank a bottle of bourbon a day and took huge doses of amphetamines. Tyler said he often saw her taking drugs, adding: 'Cocaine kept her going.'

When the accusations against Mansfield were first made by her daughter they sounded far-fetched, but later, prestigious biographer Martha Saxton reported that Jayne Marie had gone to the police in 1967 covered with bruises and other marks. She claimed she had been beaten with a leather belt at her mother's urging. No charges were brought but the girl moved out of the family home. The star's long-time press secretary, Raymond Strait, also told of her viciousness towards the child. Strait, another of her many lovers, said Jayne used to urge boyfriend Sam Brody to hurt the girl. She yelled: 'Beat her! Kill her! Black her eyes! If you love me make her bleed.'

Strait told of one occasion on which he visited Jayne and Sam at their home. He was quietly mixing himself a drink in the kitchen when he heard bloodcurdling screams. Rushing into the sitting room, he was confronted by the sight of Jayne trying to climb up the bookshelves. Said Strait: 'Her throat was filled with such screeching noises that she sounded more animal than human.' She was screaming: 'The lizards, the lizards, the f***ng

Jayne's second husband, bodybuilder Miklós 'Mickey' Hargitay.

lizards! Look at them, oh my God, look at them!' In a corner of the room crouched Brady, equally spaced out on drink and drugs. He was massaging his private parts while moaning: 'Do it baby, do it. Beautiful, eat the little pussy. Little lizards, eat the pussy!' Raymond Strait fled into the night.

Last on the list of debaucheries was the claim that Jayne held weird devil-worship ceremonies with fellow cult members in the cellar of her pink Hollywood home. Despite her belief that being involved in the occult had publicity value, the satanic rites became a bit scary and Jayne ordered the devil-worshippers out of her house. One of the spurned mystics then supposedly put a curse on her. He said she would die as a witch, either by being burned at the stake or by being decapitated.

If prophesy there ever were, it almost came true in the early hours of 29 June 1967 when, after a nightclub performance in Biloxi, Mississippi, Mansfield, along with Brody and a hired driver, Ronnie Harrison, were travelling to New Orleans for a morning TV interview. All three were riding in the front seats, with Mansfield's three children by Mickey Hargitay in the back. At 2.25 am their Buick Electra rounded a curve and, at 80 mph, slammed into and under a tractor trailer that had slowed behind a truck spraying mosquito fogger. All three front-seat passengers died instantly; the children, although suffering minor injuries, survived. The top of the car was sheared off and it was reported that Mansfield had been decapitated. This was not quite the case: although her skull was crushed, the urban myth of her decapitation was due to a police photograph showing the separated tangled remains of a blonde wig she had been wearing, possibly still attached to part of her real hair and scalp.

Jayne Mansfield was only 34 years old at the time of her death. Daughter Jayne Marie provided her mother's epitaph in typical Hollywood jargon: 'She may have been the Hitler of the sex symbol world, as far as I'm concerned. You hated to love her and loved to hate her.' Jayne Mansfield herself had previously summed up her extraordinary lifestyle somewhat more pithily: 'If you're going to do something wrong, do it big, because the punishment is the same either way.'

Jayne and her 'Tarzan': they had three children and lived in a Hollywood 'pink palace'.

Jayne in typical publicity pose beside the swimming pool of her Sunset Strip 'pink palace'.

Hargitay (left) accused his wife of an affair with movie producer Enrico Bomba (right).

Right: Jayne with her lover, singer Nelson Sardelli.

Below: Jayne, in typically dishevelled state, with third husband, film producer Matt Cimber.

Above: Jayne in 1965 with daughter Jayne Marie, who later claimed she had been abused by her mother.

Left: Dead at the age of 34: travelling to a New Orleans TV interview, Jayne's car crashed in the early hours, killing her husband Sam Brody and their driver. Her three children by Mickey Hargitay, travelling in the back, all survived.

CHAPTER NINE

Elvis Presley

Some 100,000 fans poured into town for his funeral. More than 3,000 wreaths were sent from as far afield as the Soviet Union and China. The city of Memphis erected a statue to its favourite son. Tens of thousands still tour Graceland, the home where he died. Yet despite those millions of adoring fans, hundreds of hangers-on, dozens of bodyguards and a live-in lover, on the day Elvis Presley died of a massive heart attack he lay alone on his bathroom floor for more than five hours before anyone discovered his body. The date was 16 August 1977.

Elvis was 'the King' to a rock 'n' rollin' world, but he was a sad, sick, obese wreck by the time his drug-abused body finally gave up at the age of 42. At the end, he shut himself away in his bedroom suite with its two television sets built into the ceiling. He would watch pornographic movies, some of which he had made himself while watching friends indulge in sex acts through two-way mirrors. He had also become obsessed with guns, shooting out the TV screens if he didn't like the programmes. His food fads and monumental binges had also become legendary as his girth ballooned to ugly proportions.

However, it was the drugs that killed him. Elvis took drugs to wake up, to sleep, to go to the toilet, to leave the toilet and to go on stage. The results were obvious to all but his most devoted fans; he was incoherent and often forgot the words to the songs that had made him famous. Elvis was on a roller-coaster ride to destruction. When he died, there were a total of thirteen drugs in his bloodstream.

For twenty-two years, ever since 1956, Elvis had been 'the King'. That year he released *Heartbreak Hotel, Hound Dog, Don't Be Cruel, Blue Suede Shoes* and *Love Me Tender*. The latter was also the title of his first movie, and it was the year that Elvis's first appearances on coast-to-coast television turned him into a national entertainment sensation. In 1957 he bought Graceland, a former Memphis church, upon which he

Born on 8 January 1935 in a two-room house in Tupelo, Mississippi, this is the earliest known photograph of Elvis Aaron Presley, aged 2, with mother Gladys and father Vernon.

Elvis's small-town stage performances made him a regional star from Tennessee to Texas.

Elvis with trademark quiff in 1956, the year he released *Heartbreak Hotel* and *Hound Dog*.

lavished his wealth. He also spent it unstintingly on his mother Gladys, whom he adored obsessively. When, the following year, Gladys died at the age of 46, Elvis was distraught. Recalled from military service in the US army to be with her as she sank into a coma from acute hepatitis and liver failure, Elvis rushed to the hospital and, along with his father Vernon, wept over her body. At her funeral, he said: 'Oh God, everything I have is gone. Goodbye darling, goodbye, goodbye.'

It was a trauma from which he was never to recover. Albert Goldman, author of one of the hundreds of Presley biographies, said: 'Elvis's obsession with his mother lasted throughout his life. It was an unnatural obsession that stretched beyond any normal mother-son bond and certainly accounts for many of Elvis's later sexual problems.'

Presley returned to the army, serving out his term in Germany where he had several girlfriends but in 1959 finding one on which he could lavish true love. The problem was that the object of his affection, army officer's daughter Priscilla Ann Beaulieu, was only 14 years of age. Having completed his military service, Elvis invited Priscilla to Graceland for Christmas 1960 and, after her return to Germany, realized he missed her so desperately that he pleaded with her family to allow her to finish her schooling in Memphis, under his watchful eye. A year later, they relented. Part of the agreement was that Priscilla would attend an all-girls Catholic school in Memphis and live with Elvis's

Girls threw themselves at 'the King'; here he is mobbed for autographs in 1958.

father and his stepmother in a separate house adjacent to the Graceland estate. On her graduation from the Immaculate Conception High School in June 1963, Elvis presented her with a Corvair sports car.

Elvis himself shared his time between the Memphis mansion and Hollywood, where he made twenty-one movies between 1961 and 1968. Hollywood was also where, unbeknown to Priscilla, he indulged his obsession for virginal and often under-aged girls. There might be fifty girls to eight men at the Californian court of the King but none of his so-called 'Memphis Mafia' was entitled to a companion until Elvis had taken what he called 'the pick of the litter'. Hollywood eventually soured as the films he made increasingly flopped. He turned more and more to pills, and to a degree he needed them as he was a chronic insomniac. He was stretching himself to the limit, driving across the country for twenty-four hours at a stretch and partying with a vengeance. The pills kept him going. He was taking stimulants, tranquillizers, painkillers and Quaaludes, known as a 'love drug' that improves fading sexual performance.

Elvis married his Priscilla, now 21 years of age, on 1 May 1967, and nine months later, daughter Lisa Marie was born. While his wife and child stayed at the Presleys' Californian home in Bel Air, Elvis himself spent more and more time on the road. After fallow years of movie and musical failures, his concert performances were restoring his superstar status but there was a price to pay, as bodyguard Rick Stanley revealed: 'He didn't show moderation – not just with drugs but with anything he did. When he started getting into needles in 1972 I really began to worry. He was becoming a needle-head. His body began to look like a pincushion.'

Presley needed amphetamines to boost his energy for his concerts and he needed uppers to kill his appetite. He would be injected before going on stage and again when he came off. The drugs took a toll on his mental health. His lifestyle became more bizarre. In the years before his death, he bought four planes. On a tour round Memphis one night, he bought fourteen Cadillacs and immediately gave one away to a passing stranger. A few months before his death, Elvis was waiting outside his home when he spotted a woman who resembled his beloved mother. Elvis was convinced that she was Gladys reincarnated and gave her an 18 carat gold ring that had been a gift from him to his mother.

Elvis's womanizing was equally extravagant. He regularly had his bodyguards pick a young girl from the audience after his show. She would be allowed to meet him only if she agreed to stay the night with the idol. On one occasion, Elvis almost killed himself and a girl fan, Page Peterson, with drugs. She was 18 when the star spotted her with her mother

In 1957 Presley bought his dream home, Graceland, a former church in Memphis, Tennessee.

When in 1958 his beloved mother Gladys died, aged 46, Elvis was bereft and grief-stricken.

at a Las Vegas concert. As he sung his last number, *Can't Help Falling In Love*, he could not take his eyes off her. As she later disclosed:

> A couple of minutes after the curtain came down, when everyone was still cheering, one of Elvis's helpers came up to me and asked if I wanted to meet him. I was taken to his dressing room where he talked about God and politics. He got my mother and me a hotel room but I stayed with Elvis.

Elvis sent for Page on other occasions. On one visit to him in Palm Springs, she complained of a headache and Elvis gave her some pills. She remembered nothing else. Bodyguard Sonny West heard sounds of giggling and slurred words coming from the master bedroom at 4.00 am. That was not unusual, but the following afternoon aides found the couple unconscious in the bedroom, naked and barely breathing. An ambulance took them to hospital where both had their stomachs pumped out.

> 'I remember the doctor being angry at all the drugs that were in me,' said Page. 'Elvis called my mother and a plane was sent to pick her up. I was in intensive care for two weeks. Later Elvis told me he had paid $10,000 in bribes to hush the whole thing up. He didn't come to see me because he said he would have been recognized. He did send me a verse from the Bible, though. And he did pay all the bills.'

In 1972 Priscilla walked out on Presley and they divorced the following year. Another beauty had swiftly moved into Graceland: 20-year-old 'Miss Tennessee' Linda Thompson. However, despite being deluged with an avalanche of Cadillacs, jewels, even houses for her and her parents, she too told Elvis in 1976 that she was leaving him. Linda was followed within months by another beauty contestant, Ginger Alden, who later claimed that they were engaged to be married on Christmas Day 1977. Tragically, Elvis's body would rebel before that date.

Elvis fell for Priscilla Ann Beaulieu when she was just 14.

By now, Presley was not only hiding his chronic drug-taking from his fans but was hiding himself from the world, surrounded by his Memphis Mafia of long-time buddies and bodyguards. He was buying $4,000 of pills at a time. He had a liver infection, an enlarged colon and had to wear incontinence pads to go to bed. The King held court in his bedchamber with walls of button-tufted black suede. The bed was double-king size. In the past, it had been used for many a romp, but by now he was impotent. In his clothes cupboard was a well-stocked fridge from which he gorged himself around the clock. Above it hung the $5,000 sequinned jumpsuit into which he could no longer zip himself. Beside his bed were a large photograph of his mother, a picture of Jesus Christ and a well-thumbed Bible.

In the early hours of 16 August 1977, Elvis and Ginger Alden returned to Graceland after a late-night visit to the dentist. Elvis had two fillings, while Ginger only had X-rays taken. Between 2.30 am and 4.30 am Elvis played racquetball and at 6.30 am he finally retired to bed with Ginger. The topsy-turvy timetable was thus far not unusual for the star who lived by night and slept by day. At 9.00 am Ginger awoke to find Elvis also awake. 'I'm going into the bathroom to read,' he told her. 'Don't fall asleep,' said Ginger. 'OK, I won't,' he replied.

They were the last words Elvis spoke. More than five hours later, at 2.20 pm, Ginger again woke. She sauntered through to the bathroom where she found her lover crumpled on the thickly-carpeted floor. He was rushed the short distance to Baptist Memorial Hospital where he was pronounced dead.

The Memphis state medical examiner, Dr Jerry Francisco, stated that the cause of death was 'cardiac arrhythmia' (an erratic heartbeat). He continued: 'There was severe cardiovascular disease present. He had a history of mild hypertension and some coronary

After a lengthy 'courtship', Elvis married Priscilla, then aged 21, in May 1967.

Nine months after their wedding, daughter Lisa Marie was born.

Elvis increasingly spent time away from home, mobbed by fans.

Presley's so-called 'Memphis Mafia', joined (kneeling left) by the notorious 'Dr Nick'.

There was no shortage of young female fans at venues like Las Vegas.

artery disease. Basically it was a natural death.' There was no mention of the killer drug cocktail that must have caused that erratic heartbeat. Yet only days before Elvis's death, former Memphis Mafia member Red West had written in an exposé that revealed the scale of his drug-taking:

> He takes every possible pill you can think of. He takes pills and shots for downs. He takes a very strong pain medication that is intended for terminally ill cancer patients. He takes pills that he thinks will prevent body odour. He takes pills that he thinks will give him a suntan.

Ginger Alden said she tried to stop Elvis taking drugs. She saw him take a vast pile of them on the night before he died. He told her simply: 'I need them.'

In 1979, with the scandal of the King's shameful lifestyle fully exposed, his personal physician Dr George Nichopoulos was charged with malpractice. Tennessee public health inspector Steve Belsky said in testimony: 'From my experience, Elvis Presley was issued more scheduled uppers, downers and amphetamines than any other individual I have ever seen.' It was revealed that in 1977, kindly 'Dr Nick' had prescribed Presley with 10,000 doses of amphetamines, barbiturates, narcotics, tranquillizers, sleeping pills, laxatives and hormones. He was suspended from practising for three months, charged with over-prescribing to twelve patients including Elvis and Jerry Lee Lewis. He was later acquitted by a jury and walked free.

After Elvis's divorce from Priscilla, 20-year-old Linda Thompson, a former Miss Tennessee, moved into Graceland.

Linda Thompson walked out on Presley in 1976, but was swiftly replaced by another 20-year-old beauty contestant, Ginger Alden.

His bloated body ravaged by drugs… Elvis performing in Las Vegas in 1970 (left) and in 1977.

'The King' is dead… Presley's funeral cortège passes through Memphis, watched by 100,000 fans.

CHAPTER TEN

Roman Polanski

Film director Roman Polanski had seen the horrors of war at first hand. As Jews living under the Nazi regime in Poland, his parents were removed to concentration camps and he was lucky to escape incarceration. During his later career as a film producer in the West, those childhood horrors came back to haunt him and he unsuccessfully attempted to use them as an excuse for his later dubious lifestyle and the scandal that would eventually force him into lifelong exile.

Rajmund Roman Thierry Polański was born in Paris on 18 August 1933, his family moving back to their home town of Kraków, Poland, when he was aged 4. Two years later Germany invaded and Roman spent most of the war in hiding. His mother died in Auschwitz but father and son survived and Roman became a successful film director, at first in Poland, then in Britain and finally the United States, where he cemented his reputation with the 1968 horror film *Rosemary's Baby*.

Roman Polanski appeared with Sharon Tate in his 1968 horror spoof *Dance of the Vampires*.

By now a resident of California, Polanski gained notoriety for his lifestyle through the drug-taking, sexually permissive 1960s. When in 1968 he wed the beautiful 26-year-old actress Sharon Tate, star of his horror spoof *Dance of the Vampires*, it looked as if the wild man of Hollywood might settle down. He was, after all, not just a husband but a father-to-be.

Shortly before dawn on 9 August 1969, while Polanski was in London working on a film, Tate was murdered along with four of their friends at the Polanskis' mansion in Cielo Drive, Benedict Canyon. The killers were members of the Charles Manson 'Family', whose butchery turned the stomachs of even the most hardened of Los Angeles cops. The body of Steven Parent, 18-year-old guest of the house's caretaker, was found shot in the driveway. Abigail Folger, heiress to a coffee fortune, was found lying on the lawn, cut to pieces as she tried to flee. The other bodies were found in the house. Film director Voytek Frykowski, awoken from a drugged sleep, had been hit with a club and finished off with six thrusts of a knife. Hollywood hairstylist Jay Sebring had been stabbed and then dispatched with a gunshot. The most sickening sight, however, was the pathetic body of Sharon Tate. The actress, eight months pregnant, had suffered sixteen stab wounds. Her unborn baby boy died along with her.

Roman and Sharon wed in 1968. A year later, when eight months pregnant, she and four friends were murdered at the Polanskis' Californian mansion.

Killer cult leader Charles Manson.

There was predictable public revulsion over the drugged-up killers who, along with Manson himself, were convicted of what was described as the most sickening crime of the century. However, when it was learned that Polanski and friends had been regular drug-users within the house of horror, the reaction changed. Sympathy for the film director evaporated. The American public wanted to know whether the crime was random or whether there was a link between the Manson madmen and the hippy culture enjoyed by Hollywood renegades like Polanski. Suddenly he became the story rather than the victim.

After the horrors of Cielo Drive and the recriminations that followed, Polanski, if anything, grew even wilder. The moviemaker threw himself into his work to forget his loss, but also embarked on months and years of partying and womanizing. His great friend at the time was actor Jack Nicholson and it was at the star's Los Angeles home in March 1977 that Polanski's scandalous lifestyle finally caught up with him. A French magazine wanted a glamorous spread of pictures depicting youthful beauty and Polanski, who had always had a penchant for childlike women, accepted the photographic commission with alacrity.

Polanski invited 13-year-old Samantha Gailey, whose mother may have been one of his ex-lovers, to pose for him. The photo-shoot took place around Jack Nicholson's swimming pool, although the star himself was away from home. There the director plied Samantha with champagne and the couple ended up half-naked in the Jacuzzi. Samantha testified that Polanski fed her part of a Quaalude tranquillizer, known in Hollywood as a 'love drug' because it supposedly improves sexual performance.

She said she began to feel uncomfortable after he asked her to lie down on a bed. 'I said, "No, no. I don't want to go in there. No, I don't want to do this. No, keep away" and "Come on, let's go home".' Despite her protests, Polanski then performed oral, vaginal and anal sex acts upon her. In Samantha's words, he 'went down and he started performing cuddliness'. When asked what 'cuddliness' meant, she clarified:

> He placed his mouth on my vagina. I was ready to cry. I was going, 'No. Come on. Stop it.' But we were alone and I didn't know what else would happen if I made a scene. So I was just scared, and after giving some resistance, I figured, 'Well, I guess I'll get to come home after this.'

Polanski invited 13-year-old Samantha Gailey to pose for him, then assaulted her.

Polanski's attack on the naked teenager ended when Jack Nicholson's girlfriend, Angelica Huston, turned up at the house unexpectedly. An embarrassed Samantha returned to her own home and related the night's events to her sister and mother, who phoned the police. Polanski was arrested in a room at the Beverly Wilshire Hotel. Jack Nicholson's house was searched, a small quantity of drugs found and Angelica Huston was charged with possession.

The result was that Polanski was indicted by a Grand Jury on six counts: furnishing a controlled substance to a minor; committing a lewd and lascivious act on a 13-year-old child; unlawful sexual intercourse; rape by use of drugs, including Quaalude and alcohol; perversion, including copulating by mouth with the sexual organ of the child; sodomy.

Samantha Gailey became so frightened by the attention the case attracted due to Polanski's fame that she tried to withdraw from it. The result was that her attorney consented to plea bargaining and Polanski accepted the least serious of the charges: unlawful sexual intercourse. His lawyers tried to engender sympathy for the accused by citing the horrors he had experienced as a child in war-ravaged Poland. As a sweetener for a light sentence, they also offered the court that the director would found a theatre arts school for poor children in Los Angeles.

Samantha Gailey's parents seemed mollified but the judge was not. Judge Lawrence Rittenband ruled:

> Although the prosecutrix was not an inexperienced girl, this is of course not a licence to the defendant, a man of the world in his forties, to engage in an act

Samantha's testimony was damning.

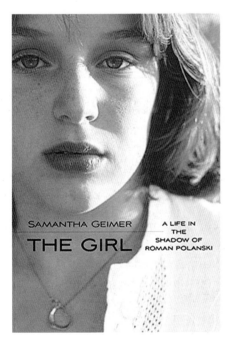

SAMANTHA GEIMER

THE GIRL

A LIFE IN THE SHADOW OF ROMAN POLANSKI

Samantha later wrote her story, under her married name Samantha Geimer.

of unlawful sexual intercourse with her. The law was designed for the protection of females under the age of 18 years, and it is no defence to such a charge that the female might not have resisted the act.

Polanski was ordered to spend ninety days undergoing psychiatric tests at a state institution, along with other inmates that he disdainfully dismissed as 'the scum of society'. After that, he was again to face the judge to receive his full sentence. Polanski confidently anticipated a deal whereby he would eventually walk from court scot-free. Meanwhile, he served out only part of his ninety days before getting permission to make a series of trips to Paris to work on film projects. This infuriated Judge Rittenband, especially as, while supposedly making preparations for the case, the roaming director was flaunting a fresh teen love affair with 16-year-old starlet Nastassja Kinski. Polanski's lawyers warned him that the judge was planning to disregard the plea bargain and sentence Polanski to fifty years in prison, having been heard to vow: 'I'll see this man never gets out of jail.'

On the day before sentencing, Polanski fled the country. Since he had already travelled several times from Los Angeles to France without being stopped by the authorities, he quietly boarded a night flight to Paris on 31 January 1978. There, as a French-born citizen, he was safe from extradition. Disgusted, Rittenband transferred the case to another judge. The papers were filed away to gather dust, although the charges remained pending.

From his European refuge, Polanski gave interviews in which he tried to defend his actions, saying that he had always been attracted to 'young girls' and was 'incredulous' that he should have been arrested for rape. He declared: 'Judges want to fuck young girls. Juries want to fuck young girls. Everyone wants to fuck young girls!' Polanski himself has written about his sexual predilection for juveniles. In his 1984 autobiography *Roman by Polanski*, he admitted: 'I am widely regarded, I know, as an evil, profligate dwarf.' However, he explained away his seduction of Samantha Gailey as no more than a date. 'I asked when she had first started having sex,' he wrote, as if that were a normal conversational gambit by a 43-year-old man to a 13-year-old girl. He added: 'We weren't saying much but I could sense a certain erotic tension between us.'

In 1993 Polanski's victim, now married and going by the name of Samantha Geimer, settled a lawsuit against him in which she had alleged sexual assault, false imprisonment, seduction of a minor and intentional infliction of emotional distress. The terms of settlement, believed to be $500,000, were not disclosed and it was unclear from court filings what sum was ever paid and why the case was not pursued further. In 1997 Geimer publicly forgave Polanski and unsuccessfully began advocating that the rape charge against him be dropped.

The case for Polanski has not been helped by other historic claims that have followed. In 2010 British actress Charlotte Lewis said Polanski had 'forced himself' on her in 1983 when, at the age of 16, she was auditioning for a role in Paris. In 2017 more claimants came forward, including the following: US former actress Mallory Millett who accused Polanski of trying to rape her when he was high on LSD in 1970; German ex-actress Renate Langer who said she was raped when she was 15 in 1972; a Californian named only as Robin M. who said she was 'sexually victimized' when she was 16 in 1973; and, most seriously, Californian artist Marianne Barnard who alleged she was assaulted in 1975 when she was only 10 years old. As a celebrity refugee, Polanski continued to protest his innocence while still resisting US extradition attempts from his self-imposed banishment.

In 1993 Samantha Geimer settled a lawsuit against Polanski and in 1997 publicly forgave him.

Polanski with Jack Nicholson and Angelica Huston. The sex attack was at the actor's home.

Polanski leaves court in October 1997. The following January he quietly fled the country.

Living it up abroad: surrounded by pretty girls at the 1977 Munich Oktoberfest…

… and with his teenage lover Nastassja Kinski at the Paris première of his 1979 film *Tess*.

Charlotte Lewis, seen here with Polanski in Cannes in 1986, claimed he 'forced himself' on her.

Mallory Millett accused Polanski of trying to rape her when he was high on LSD in 1970.

Renate Langer claimed that Polanski raped her in 1972 when she was just 15.

Artist Marianne Barnard alleged he assaulted her when she was aged just 10.

CHAPTER ELEVEN

Joan Crawford

With the title *Mommie Dearest*, the book written by the adopted daughter of actress Joan Crawford might have led readers to expect a paean of praise for one of Hollywood's most fabled superstars. Nothing could have been further from the truth. Christina Crawford's 1978 blockbuster painted a nightmare picture of life with a viciously abusive mother. The book described unbalanced alcoholic rages, violent attacks and cruel mind games played on Crawford's children. It catalogued a string of affairs that the star enjoyed with both men and women. It even hinted that she had tried to kill one of her husbands.

Joan Crawford's own abused and unhappy upbringing may partly explain her maltreatment of her own family. Born Lucille Fay LeSueur in 1904 in San Antonio, Texas, she was the illegitimate daughter of a poverty-stricken mother and a roving father who abandoned the family a few months before her birth. Her mother then married a minor opera

house impresario and moved to Lawton, Oklahoma, where Lucille was beaten regularly and put to work before she was 10 years old. Her stepfather, who she believed to be her biological parent, reportedly began sexually abusing her from the age of 11 until she was freed from his clutches by being sent away to a Catholic academy in Kansas City.

In her late teens, Lucille began dancing in the choruses of travelling revues and was spotted by a producer, Jacob J. Shubert, who gave the 20-year-old a job in the chorus line of his Broadway shows. F. Scott Fitzgerald described her as 'the best example of the flapper' but she must have been better than that because an MGM talent scout spotted her and she was signed up by the studio. The only snag was that she had just made a blue movie, which MGM had to buy from a blackmailer to protect her image. They also changed her name from LeSueur (which the studio's publicist said sounded like a 'sewer') to Joan Crawford.

The budding star moved to Hollywood and vowed never to be poor or lonely again. She avoided the latter by regularly inviting a selection of unaccompanied males to dinner and choosing one of them to stay the night. In a reversal of Hollywood roles, it was she who would audition her own leading men by a session on the casting couch.

Crawford had already had one serious relationship: while still on Broadway in 1924, she had moved in with a saxophone player, James Welton, to whom she was rumoured to have gone through a form of marriage ceremony, although this was never mentioned by her in later life. Her first 'official' marriage was much more celebrated. In 1929 she wed actor Douglas Fairbanks Jr, much to the displeasure of his father Fairbanks Sr and stepmother Mary Pickford, who both boycotted the wedding. The couple longed for children but by the time she became pregnant, the marriage had broken down and she obtained an abortion, claiming to her husband that she had miscarried. Before ending the marriage in 1933, citing 'grievous mental cruelty' and 'a jealous and suspicious attitude', the actress had begun an affair with Clark Gable, himself married at the time. It is even likely that the child she terminated was Gable's. The lovers appeared in eight films together and carried on their affair intermittently for two decades, remaining close until his death in

Lucille Fay LeSueur aged 6.

1960. As Crawford later told her biographer Charlotte Chandler in *Not the Girl Next Door*:

> Clark was all man. I've been asked many times about him and what was so attractive about him. I can tell you, and I can tell you in one word if you won't be shocked: Balls! Clark Gable had balls. There were people who said we were having an affair. Well, they could say what they wanted, but the source of the information wasn't me and it wasn't Clark. We weren't that kind of people. And I never saw any witnesses in the bedroom.

Crawford is also quoted in the biography *Clark Gable* by Chrystopher J. Spicer:

> We were attracted to each other instantly. I had what he wanted and he had what I wanted. Call it chemistry, call it love at first sight, call it physical attraction. What's the difference? The electricity between us sparked on screen. It wasn't just acting; we meant every damn kiss and embrace. God, we both had balls in those days!

The early 1930s were the golden years for Joan Crawford. Her movies, such as *Forsaking All Others* with Clark Gable and *Dancing Lady* with Gable and Fred Astaire, were among the most popular and highest-grossing of the era. A 1932 Hollywood poll of 'Top Moneymaking Stars' put her third in popularity.

Joan Crawford as a young actress.

In 1935 Crawford wed husband number two, actor Franchot Tone, who had also appeared with her in *Dancing Lady*, but the marriage lasted only four years. Again they tried for babies but Joan suffered two miscarriages and was told she could no longer bear children. She stormed out of the marital home when she found Tone in bed with another actress, even though she herself was having an affair with actor Spencer Tracy.

Husband number three was a minor actor named Phillip Terry, who she wed in 1942 after a six-week courtship. The marital routine she set her new husband was eccentric, including him in the daily schedule she drew up for her domestic staff and devoting exactly an hour and a half for sex every evening. Two years earlier, Joan had adopted a baby girl, initially called Joan but who she renamed Christina, and it is probable that the only reason she married Terry was to give the child a stable home life. Once wed, the couple adopted another baby, a boy they called Phillip Terry Jr. However, as Joan became increasingly bored with her less-famous husband, this marriage also began to fail. When they divorced in 1946, the young Phillip Terry Jr was renamed Christopher Crawford. Joan went on to adopt two more children named Cathy and Cindy in 1947. Throughout her life, she referred to them as 'the twins'. This mystified many acquaintances since the children came from different families, were different ages and looked nothing like one another.

By now, Crawford's behaviour had become increasingly bizarre as she launched herself into a string of fresh affairs. At the age of 50, her body was still that of a nubile young girl and she loved to show it off. Her dates would turn up to find her in nothing more than skimpy lingerie. She once turned up at the home of a new director, Charles Walters, stark naked. Flinging off her housecoat as he answered the door, she announced: 'I think you should see what you have to work with!'

Crawford married her fourth and final husband in 1955, giving her a new and unlikely corporate image. He was Alfred Steele, president of Pepsi-Cola, who sent her off touring the world to promote his product. Steele died of a heart attack in 1959 but his widow was given a seat on the board as she continued her promotional role for the company for a further fourteen years. Pepsi-Cola had never been Joan's favourite tipple but when endorsing the fizzy product, she claimed it was all she drank. Preferring the harder stuff, her innocent-looking ice-box was packed with liquor and her glass of Pepsi was usually laced with a liberal slug of vodka. When booking into a hotel, her room bar would be stocked with her regular order of 'Two bottles of 100 proof Smirnoff vodka, a bottle of Old Forester bourbon, a bottle of Beefeater gin and two bottles of Dom Perignon champagne.'

Joan's hard drinking was part of the problem that beset her own family life and caused the eventual backlash by her adopted daughter that trashed her reputation forever. A year after Crawford's death from stomach cancer in 1977 at the age of 73, the bombshell biography *Mommie Dearest* was published. In it, Christina described the vicious beatings her mother gave her and her three adopted siblings. She would tie them to their beds if they sucked their thumbs. She would make them scrub the floors repeatedly for no reason. She would have the same food served up meal after meal if any of the children failed to finish their portion.

Christina described how Crawford would come storming into the children's bedroom in a drunken fury and smash everything in sight; how an endless succession of 'uncles' were invited to stay; how she was once starved for days when she refused to eat an undercooked steak; how she was sent away to school and did not see her mother for a year at a time.

She wrote graphically of her mother's alcoholic rages: 'Grabbing for my throat like a mad dog, with a look in her eyes that will never be erased from my memory. Her eyes were the eyes of a killer animal.' Aged 13, she suffered a brutal beating from her mother in which she thought she was going to be choked to death. After Joan married Alfred Steele, Christina suffered one final attack when she made the mistake of kissing her new stepfather goodnight. Her mother hit her hard, saying: 'I got my man, now you damn well go out and get your own.' Although Christina never accused her mother of trying to dispose of Steele, she pointed to the fact that the healthy man 'suspiciously' fell down the stairs only three years after they had been married.

Christina wrote that when she was 15 she was so depressed from her mother's treatment towards her that she tried to kill herself at boarding school by overdosing on pills. Her mother was told of the suicide bid, but never contacted her or ever spoke of the incident.

Christina also wrote about ill-treatment towards her brother Christopher. Crawford

The young Hollywood beauty wed heartthrob Douglas Fairbanks Jr in 1929.

The men in her arms: Clark Gable in *Possessed* in 1931, second husband Franchot Tone in 1935, and Spencer Tracy in *Mannequin* in 1937.

Above: Third husband Phillip Terry. She scheduled exactly ninety minutes for sex with him each evening.

Right: Fourth husband Alfred Steele.

In 1940 Crawford adopted a baby girl, initially called Joan but later renamed Christina. As a teenager, she claimed she was so cruelly treated that she attempted suicide. In 1978 she wrote the bombshell memoir mockingly titled *Mommie Dearest*.

SURVIVOR
—— A MEMOIR ——
Christina Crawford
#1 *NEW YORK TIMES*–BESTSELLING
AUTHOR OF *MOMMIE DEAREST*

supposedly kept him tied up in bed in a 'sleep safe' device, while Christina was often trussed up in the shower at night. Christopher, she said, ran away from home four times.

Her brother also spoke venomously of their mother. 'I hated the bitch,' he said. 'She was evil. I know that's a terrible thing to say, but it's the truth.' Christopher, a 6ft 4in Vietnam veteran, recalled how when he was 5 his sister dressed him up in some of their mother's clothes. 'We were just playing but she went berserk. She whipped and whipped me with an army belt.' He said his mother once taught him a lesson for playing with matches by holding his hand in the fire. His blisters took months to heal.

After the publication of *Mommie Dearest*, later adapted into a movie starring Faye Dunaway, two of her family came to her defence. Her adopted daughters Cathy and Cindy, who grew up in the same house during much the same years, denied Christina's and Christopher's allegations. Cathy said: 'My mother was not *Mommie Dearest* as shown in the book. I have never met that person. My mother was a warm, caring human being and I will miss her all my life.' Cindy added:

> I always knew Christina hated mother. I understand that she had been writing that book for years. She had almost finished when our mother died. Quick as a wink, she revised the thing with extra venom. In my opinion, she has done an immoral thing which some day she will answer for.

Sure enough, answer for it she did. In Joan Crawford's will, two of the four children were excluded. The actress wrote: 'It is my intention to make no provision herein for my son Christopher or my daughter Christina for reasons which are well known to them.'

Joan Crawford was one of the screen's longest-reigning stars. She made eighty films in a forty-year career, was labelled 'Queen of the Movies', enjoyed a harem of male lovers, was married four times and ended up as a director of the giant Pepsi-Cola corporation. Yet her entire reputation was destroyed by one 'tell all' memoir written by the daughter who could not bring herself to forgive the meanness of the parent she mockingly called 'Mommie Dearest'.

When Crawford died in 1977, she was lauded as 'Queen of the Movies'. A year later, her reputation was destroyed by her daughter's revelations.

CHAPTER TWELVE

Rock Hudson

The world's press was gathered outside the American Hospital in Paris. Inside was one of Hollywood's greatest heart-throbs; a sex symbol envied by men and idolized by women. What, everyone wanted to know, was wrong with Rock Hudson? Eventually his publicist emerged to announce: 'Mr Hudson has Acquired Immune Deficiency Syndrome. It was diagnosed over a year ago in the United States.' There was a moment of shocked silence. Then the reporters raced to telephones to tell the world that the 59-year-old hunk, who had played the role of lover to some of the screen's most beautiful women, was the first major celebrity to succumb to what was then reprovingly known as the 'Gay Plague'. It was to be a shocking, humiliating and pitiful end for one of movieland's most dashing heroes.

Rock Hudson's entire adult life had been a lie. Born plain Roy Harold Scherer on 17 November 1925, he grew up with the abandoned mother he adored and a stepfather he hated. He left his home town of Winnetka, Illinois, to spend two years in the US navy, serving in the Philippines before heading for the sparkling lights of Hollywood, where he found work as a truck driver and vacuum cleaner salesman while seeking a career

in the film business. However, it was his sexuality rather than his acting talent that got him his big break. The aspiring actor was spotted by openly gay Henry Willson, a talent scout for the David O. Selznick studio, who renamed his discovery Rock Hudson after the Rock of Gibraltar and the Hudson River. 'I was impressed by his size,' said Willson enigmatically.

The legend had been born, but the myth of the Adonis, the lady-killer with strapping masculinity, had to be sustained. It was not easy. Studio chiefs went to amazing lengths to disguise Rock Hudson's many sexual liaisons. In 1953 Rock, who had appeared in several movies but was not yet considered top billing, met 22-year-old Jack Navaar and within days they became live-in lovers. Rock was now signed to Universal Studios which, seeing him as a superstar in the ascendancy, grew ever more cautious about any bad publicity that might damage its investment. When his major movie *Magnificent Obsession* premièred, both

Sailor boy: Roy Harold Scherer spent two years in the US navy.

Rock and Jack turned up at the ceremony with female escorts organized by the studio.

Hudson's sex life remained rampant, however. When the Hollywood scandal sheet *Confidential* threatened to expose his bed-hopping affairs, Universal ordered him to clean up his act. He vainly promised to remain celibate but, just in case he didn't, a plan was worked out to turn the promiscuous homosexual into a happily married man! The studio chose as the 'lucky bride' his agent's secretary Phyllis Gates, who went to the altar on 9 November 1955 unaware that her bridegroom was gay and that the entire marriage was a set-up. Thereafter, Phyllis was utterly frustrated and perplexed by Hudson's lack of sexual interest in her. She even consulted a psychiatrist who suggested she wear frilly underwear to seduce her husband. An even sadder side to their relationship emerged after his death, when she revealed that he would cruelly ignore her for weeks and that he would occasionally beat her. When she decided to seek a divorce, she consulted top show-business lawyer Jerry Giesler and it was only then that she learned the truth about her sham marriage. Giesler said Rock himself had come to him to talk about the threat of exposure and had hinted at the cruel deception that could avert it. Phyllis was left so heartbroken that she never married again and she was a virtual recluse when, aged 80, she died of lung cancer in 2006.

None of this surfaced at the time, of course, and Rock's career continued to soar above most other stars. By 1959, when he made the memorable comedy *Pillow Talk* with his good friend Doris Day, Hudson was one of the world's biggest box office attractions.

Henry Wilson (left) was an openly gay talent scout who spotted the aspiring actor and renamed his discovery Rock Hudson after the Rock of Gibraltar and the Hudson River.

However, as his career hit the stratosphere, he forgot his promises of self-discipline and, as he later admitted, thought about sex constantly, even when rehearsing his lines or driving to the studio. Thoughts became deeds. His libido was said to be so strong that he could have sex sessions with several people several times a day. When he entertained at his Beverly Hills estate, known as 'The Castle', he would have several handsome young men frolicking in the pool for his selection.

Among them was a young film extra named Lee Garlington, then aged 24, who met the actor on the Universal Studios lot in 1962 and subsequently got a call from one of Hudson's friends inviting him to The Castle:

> 'I think he'd had me checked out,' recalled Garlington. 'When I arrived, he offered me a beer and said, "Well, let's get together" and we did. I'd come over after work, spend the night and leave the next morning. I'd sneak out at 6am and coast down the street without turning on the engine so the neighbours wouldn't hear. We thought we were being so clever. He was a sweetheart and I adored him.'

During their three-year affair, the pair attended film premières together, although each brought along a female 'date'.

Sham marriage: Rock's 'lucky bride' in 1955 was his agent's secretary Phyllis Gates.

Rock at a 1956 studio event with (from left) movie mogul Jack Warner, actress Natalie Wood, Henry Wilson and Phyllis, still unaware that her husband was gay.

A screen kiss for Elizabeth Taylor in *Giant* (1956).

In 1973 publicist Tom Clark moved into The Castle. Clark was a far cry from the pretty-faced men usually courted by Hudson but he enjoyed the same hobbies of football, cooking and travelling and became the great love of the star's life. As a bonus, for the first time Hudson could actually take a man with him everywhere he wished, for Tom had become the actor's publicist. The lovers hosted many lavish parties at the estate, including one for Rock's 50th birthday in 1975, when the star walked down the staircase clad only in a nappy while the band played *You Must Have Been a Beautiful Baby*. 'It was,' the star recalled, 'the prettiest party we ever had.'

Other parties were not so 'pretty'. A dozen or so of the couple's closest friends would be invited for orgies involving anything up to fifty attractive young men. At one, Rock appraised a particular hunk and said: 'Look at that – on a scale of one to ten, he's eleven.' As the 1980s dawned, Rock's love of parties and his growing love of the bottle were taking their toll on his health and his appearance. For a while, he moved to San Francisco where he toured the gay bars, picking up partners indiscriminately. In 1983, having tired of long-time lover Clark, a new partner, 29-year-old Marc Christian, was given the run of the mansion. It was clear to friends that not only were they lovers but that Rock was in love. It was a stormy relationship, however, and there were long spells when neither Marc nor Rock would be speaking to one another.

If Hudson's love life was in a mess, so was his movie career as his looks began to betray his debauched lifestyle. He took a regular role in the television saga *Dynasty* in which, during one now-infamous scene, he indulged in a long and lingering kiss with co-star Linda Evans. By now he knew he had AIDS but selfishly he wasn't telling anyone, not even Marc Christian.

In August 1984 Rock flew to France, telling Marc that he was visiting the Deauville Film Festival. That was true, but the real reason for his trip was to consult a Paris clinic that was experimenting with a new AIDS drug. The star took the treatment and persuaded himself that he was cured. Within months, however, his weight loss was giving his friends cause for alarm, yet he still tried to hide his illness from Marc, who asked him outright: 'Do you have AIDS?' Rock replied coolly: 'No. I've been checked for everything including the plague and I don't have it.'

It was not until February 1985 that Hudson finally admitted to a horrified Marc that he had the disease, and then only passed the message to him through his secretary.

Doris Day was not only a co-star but a great friend when they made the hit film *Pillow Talk*.

'Look after the boy,' said Hudson. 'I may have killed him.' In July of that year, Rock flew to Paris for treatment. He was so weak that he collapsed in his suite at the Ritz Hotel and was rushed to the American Hospital. From there, he authorized the statement finally admitting his condition. Marc heard the shock announcement on the six o'clock TV news.

The pathetically thin Rock Hudson was flown back to Los Angeles on a chartered jet, from which he was removed by stretcher in the dead of night. His wraith-like frame was taken by helicopter to the University of California Medical Center, but there was little the specialists could do. Reunited with Marc back at The Castle, he took short walks beside the pool and would gaze out over the city that had fuelled his early dreams. As his condition worsened, he watched old movies to remind himself of his golden age.

Finally, his once-strapping frame deathly thin and covered with sores, Rock could not even manage to sit up in bed unaided. His ex-lover and greatest friend Tom Clark returned to The Castle. Actress Liz Taylor was also a regular visitor. A priest also visited the estate, gave Rock communion and took his confession. On the morning of 2 October 1985 the star awoke early. A nurse dressed him with difficulty because he was receiving nourishment through an intravenous

drip. Clark watched over him and realized that his condition was worsening. He undressed him again and put him back to bed. Within half an hour, he was dead.

The scandals surrounding Rock Hudson's demise failed to die with him. Marc Christian, cut out of the star's will, launched a lawsuit against his estate, claiming that his lover, friends and doctors had withheld potentially life-saving information. 'I moved into Rock Hudson's house and trusted him,' Marc told a court, 'I want justice.' In 1991 an appeals court upheld a $5 million award to Marc to compensate for the fear of his developing AIDS, which a judge described as 'the ultimate in personal horror'.

Kisses for Doris Day in their 1959 movie *Pillow Talk* (top) and *Lover Come Back* in 1961.

Gay and promiscuous, Hudson
nevertheless 'enjoyed' intimate movie
clinches with unsuspecting actresses
Gina Lollobrigida (above in the
1961 film *Come September*) and Julie
Andrews (*Darling Lili* in 1970).

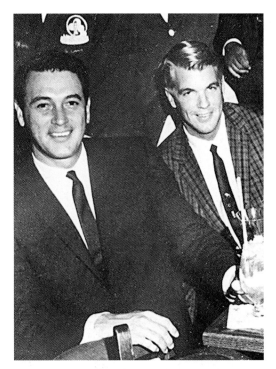

Rock (below) at his Beverly Hills estate, known as 'The Castle', where he would have several young men frolicking in the pool for his selection. A favourite was Lee Garlington (left) with whom he had a three-year affair during which they attended Hollywood events together, but each accompanied by female 'dates'.

Marc Christian, the star's long-term lover, asked him in August 1984 whether he was suffering from AIDS and was assured: 'I don't have it.' The following October, Rock Hudson was dead.

CHAPTER THIRTEEN

Jim Bakker & Jimmy Swaggart

Only in America could religious leaders attain the celebrity status of TV stars, and few raised themselves so high – in their own estimation, if not the Lord's – than Jim Bakker, a self-appointed holy man with some pretty unholy habits. The glitzy evangelist would have been familiar with the Bible warning: 'The Lord giveth and the Lord taketh away.' So the hot gospeller should not have been surprised that the Lord, having giveth him far too much, eventually had to taketh it ALL away.

Throughout the 1980s' boom in 'televangelism' in America, Bakker reached the very top of his vocation by a tear-stained style of Bible-thumping that had the viewers sending in untold millions of dollars. Peak earning time was the *Jim and Tammy Show*, an extraordinary double-act of syrupy sweetness and light with his blonde, bronzed, mascara-daubed wife. Born James Orsen Bakker in Muskegon, Michigan on 2 January 1940, Bakker had married Tamara Faye LaValley in 1961 while they were Bible students at North Central University in Minneapolis. Ordained in 1964, he set off with Tammy on the path to glory by working at the Christian Broadcasting Network, hosting a daily children's show called *Come on Over* which was an immediate success.

In 1972 they went the way of so many show business hopefuls by moving to California to head up an organization called PTL. It stood for 'Praise the Lord' but it also spelled easy money for the schmaltzy TV twosome. Two years later, the Bakkers relocated to Charlotte, North Carolina, and began their own show, *The PTL Club*, which was a phenomenal success, picked up by almost 100 stations with an average viewing figure of more than 12 million. At the height of their ministry, the Bakkers were watched by 13.5million people across America.

Perma-tanned preachers Jim and Tammy Bakker.

Abandoned dreams: Heritage USA was billed as a 'Christian-themed retreat and gospel park'.

What he lacked in stature, Jim Bakker made up for in evangelical charisma. He preached, he appealed and, of course, the money rolled in. By the early 1980s, Jim and Tammy had built a theme park with shopping mall and hotel at Fort Mills, South Carolina. Officially described as a 'Christian-themed retreat and gospel park', others dubbed it 'Christian Disneyland'. Titled Heritage USA, the 2,300-acre park attracted 6 million visitors a year and briefly became the third most successful park in America, at one point grossing $130 million annually. They also had a satellite system that distributed their network twenty-four hours a day across 1,200 channels. Contributions from the Bakkers' devoted followers were estimated at more than $1 million a week.

If anyone criticized the televangelical bandwagon, Bakker would respond: 'I believe that if Jesus were alive today he would be on TV.' In fact, if Jesus were alive, he certainly would not have approved of this greedy, seedy hypocrite. For this minister hid a secret from his generous flock: he had taken a church secretary, Jessica Hahn, to a hotel in Clearwater Beach, Florida, in 1980. Bakker allegedly drugged and had sex with Jessica, pinning her down for an hour as he raped her, repeatedly telling her: 'By helping the shepherd, you are helping the sheep.' He then said a short prayer before returning to the pulpit to admonish his flock for not following God's ways. It was a particularly unsavoury one-night stand that remained secret for seven years until revealed in March 1987. At the same time, Tammy Bakker's on-off dependency on drugs also came to light.

Jessica Hahn claimed that Bakker drugged and raped her, after which he said a short prayer.

When the scandals broke, Jim Bakker denied allegations of rape but did admit to meeting the woman in the hotel room. However, he claimed that he was the victim of a 'diabolical plot' to oust him from his seat of power and alleged that he had been 'wickedly manipulated' for the benefit of 'treacherous former friends'. This was a thinly-veiled hint that his television rival, Jimmy Swaggart, was jealous of his supreme position as America's Number One TV evangelist. Indeed, Swaggart had recently unleashed fire and brimstone against him over the Jessica Hahn incident and, interviewed on the *Larry King Show*, had called him a 'cancer in the body of Christ'.

Jim Bakker resigned in order to fight these irreligious slurs, leaving colleague Jerry Falwell to run PTL as a caretaker until he and Tammy were able to return to take their rightful place. Falwell was made of sterner stuff, however. He dug into PTL's dealings and discovered a black hole of funds being sucked into the Bakkers' personal accounts. It was also revealed that the pair, who travelled in 'his and hers' Rolls Royces, owned a vast Florida condominium, complete with $60,000 gold fixtures, which the preacher had described as a 'parsonage'. There was also the question of more than a quarter of a million dollars paid into an account to which Miss Hahn had access; it sounded very much like hush money.

While Jim and Tammy Bakker were off the air, supposedly marshalling their defence against these scurrilous allegations, they appealed to Jerry Falwell for a subsistence

Preacher Jerry Falwell uncovered a massive fraud.   Tears of a hypocrite as Bakker is arrested.

allowance. Falwell was astonished at their 'shopping list' of demands: $300,000 a year for him, $100,000 for her, a lakeside home in South Carolina, fees for attorneys, wages for security guards and a maid, plus further luxurious perks. 'I don't see any repentance there,' said Falwell. 'I see greed, the self-centredness, the avarice that brought them down.' He publicly decried Bakker as a liar, embezzler, sexual deviant and 'the greatest scab and cancer on the face of Christianity in 2,000 years of church history.'

At Bakker's fraud trial, it was revealed that money raised to spread the good word had been spread extra thinly to allow the phoney prophet to siphon off almost $5 million, along with a $279,000 pay-off for Jessica Hahn's silence. Bakker, who seemingly made all the financial decisions for his organization, kept two sets of books to conceal the accounting irregularities. Bakker and his attorney, the Reverend Richard Dortch, were defrocked from the PTL church in May 1987. The ensuing scandal went into overdrive as Hahn posed nude for *Playboy* magazine before becoming a saucy chat-line DJ, while Bakker became the subject of a government inquiry into his fund-raising gimmicks.

Retribution was slow in coming but in August 1989 Dortch, having agreed to testify at the forthcoming Bakker trial, was jailed for eight years. Bakker, meanwhile, was still to be seen in public, making tearful appearances before the television cameras as he was wheeled back and forth for psychiatric tests. The Bakker trial itself suffered further delay when the preacher was found cowering like a whipped cur on the floor of his lawyer's office. By way of defence, the lawyer involved assured the court that his client was 'a man of love, compassion and character who cares for his fellow man'. The judge

Left: Divorced from Tammy, Bakker wed Lori Graham.

Below: Bakker, with second wife Lori, returned to the TV evangelism business after his term in prison.

was unimpressed and, after a five-week trial in Charlotte, Bakker was found guilty on all counts. He was sentenced to a $500,000 fine and forty-five years in jail. For once at least, the tears that flowed down his cheeks were perhaps warranted.

In early 1991, a federal appeals court upheld Bakker's conviction on the fraud and conspiracy charges but voided his forty-five-year sentence, together with the $500,000 fine. A new jail term was set at eight years and he was granted parole in 1995 after serving just five.

Jim and Tammy Bakker divorced in 1992. She went on to marry his best friend, Roe Messner, and died in 2007. Bakker married again in 1998 to Lori Beth Graham. He moved to Branson, Missouri, where he returned to the evangelism business, broadcasting a new daily *Jim Bakker Show*. In a supposedly confessional book, *I Was Wrong*, he admitted that the first time he had read the Bible all the way through had been in prison. He wrote: 'I was appalled that I could have been so wrong and I was deeply grateful that God had not struck me dead as a false prophet!'

*   *   *

If lightning were to strike twice, this was the occasion that it could reasonably have been construed as an act of heavenly judgement. For the rival preacher who the corrupt Jim Bakker had first blamed for his downfall (as reported in the previous section) was doomed to suffer a similar fate, and fellow television evangelist Jimmy Swaggart's demise was equally scandalous.

Swaggart was a braggart, boasting that, unlike Bakker, he was incorruptible. Most of his flock believed him, until they heard what he got up to in a seedy New Orleans motel room. The evidence was in the form of photographs handed to officials from his Assemblies of God church showing Swaggart taking a prostitute, Debra Murphree, into the motel.

Swaggart's downfall was sweet revenge for yet another rival TV evangelist, Martin Gorman, who had also been defrocked after Swaggart accused him of 'immoral dalliances' in 1986. Gorman, who ran a successful TV show from New Orleans, had launched an unsuccessful $90 million lawsuit against Swaggart for spreading false rumours. In revenge, he had hired a private detective to follow his persecutor. He discovered that Debra Murphree was regularly employed by Swaggart to perform obscene sex acts while he watched from the comfort of an armchair. Murphree went along with the lucrative sex games until the preacher suggested that she invite her 9-year-old daughter to watch too. The mother, who had a record of prostitution offences in two states, announced that she was so disgusted that she felt obliged to go public with her story. She recreated Swaggart's favourite poses for *Penthouse* magazine, and the sixteen pages of explicit pictures were deemed so hot that they had to be sealed in each issue. Murphree also went on a national media tour to publicize her revelations.

Swaggart resigned from his ministry in 1988. With his long-suffering wife Frances at his side, he sobbed in front of a congregation of 7,000 in Baton Rouge, Louisiana, and confessed to 'moral failure', adding: 'I do not plan in any way to whitewash my sin or call it a mistake.' Turning to Frances, he said: 'I have sinned against you and I beg your forgiveness.'

It could have been the end for Swaggart, who had been introduced to religious fanaticism at an early age by his Pentecostal evangelist parents, Sun and Minnie Belle. Born

Braggart Jimmy Swaggart attacked his TV evangelist rival Bakker, but proved equally corruptible.

on 15 March 1935 in Ferriday, Louisiana, Jimmy Lee Swaggart was as precocious as his cousin, the rock and roll phenomenon Jerry Lee Lewis. Jimmy sang and preached on street corners and led congregations when he was only 9 years old. He married when he was just 17 and went on the road as a full-time travelling preacher. In the 1960s he recorded gospel music albums while building up another audience via Christian-themed radio stations. In the 1970s he switched to television with *The Jimmy Swaggart Telecast*, which, at its height, was broadcast on 300 channels in the US and repeated in more than 100 other countries. By the mid-1980s he had become America's most popular TV preacher.

On the face of it, the singing evangelist had not put a foot wrong in life until he fell for the charms of Debra Murphree. Because of such perfectly understandable 'moral sins', Swaggart's local church, the compassionate Louisiana Assemblies of God, was inclined to deal with him leniently and recommended a minimal three-month suspension from preaching. The national church was hardly much tougher and ordered him banished from the pulpit for a full year. Swaggart, however, unwisely defied the ban after only a few months on the grounds that his absence would destroy his $140 million-a-year worldwide ministries. He was immediately defrocked by the Assemblies of God.

Murphree faded from the scene after a proposed movie deal about her meetings with the dirty preacher failed to come to fruition. Swaggart, meanwhile, saw his television empire dwindle from tens of millions of viewers to mere thousands. The self-appointed mouthpiece of the Lord was merciful towards himself, telling his congregation that God had forgiven him for his sins, adding piously: 'What's past is past.'

In 1991 Swaggart was stopped by a police officer in Indio, California, for driving his car erratically and was discovered to be sharing it with a prostitute and a pile of porn magazines. His companion, Rosemary Garcia, said Swaggart had stopped to proposition her as she stood at the roadside. She later told reporters: 'He asked me for sex. I mean, that's why he stopped me. That's what I do. I'm a prostitute.' This time, rather than confessing to his congregation, Swaggart brazened it out with the rebuff: 'The Lord told me it's flat none of your business.'

Swaggart took prostitute Debra Murphree to a seedy motel room.

Debra Murphree went on television to describe her paid-for tryst with Swaggart.

Swaggart made a tearful television appearance piously claiming that God had forgiven him.

This mischievous plaque marks where Swaggart picked up a prostitute at a Californian roadside.

CHAPTER FOURTEEN

Woody Allen

More than twenty-five years elapsed before Dylan Farrow's anguished claims of sexual abuse were taken seriously by Hollywood. Her sense of anger and despair was all the more acute because her story had been repeated again and again to a film industry that wasn't listening. It took a latter-day scandal about 'casting couch' predators to bring to the fore Dylan's shocking allegation: that she had been molested as a 7-year-old child by her own adoptive father, the famed actor and director Woody Allen. Only when Hollywood was convulsed by a fresh frenzy of abuse scandals in 2017 were Dylan's claims finally endorsed.

The reasons why had it taken a quarter of a century for his daughter's claims to shatter Woody Allen's reputation are not hard to fathom. To his peers in Hollywood and to his millions of fans around the world, Allen was a cinematic genius. With his comic acting, witty scripts and sophisticated directing, he was almost a one-man film industry, churning out a movie every year of his long career. His power and money had 'historically protected him', said his accuser when relaunching her claims in 2018. However, the main problem Dylan had faced over the years was not Allen's fame but the near-impossibility of disentangling the truth from a vicious war of words between him and Dylan's mother, actress Mia Farrow.

The couple's relationship had left a poisonous legacy but Woody Allen's love life has never been serene. Born Allan Stewart Konigsberg in Brooklyn, New York, in 1935, Woody wooed his first wife, Harlene Rosen, when he was 19 and she was just 16. Their marriage was stormy and after their bitter split in 1959, Harlene took out legal action because the young comic cruelly referred to her in his nightclub act as 'Quasimodo'. His second marriage, to actress Louise Lasser in 1966, was initially joyful but also ended in divorce three years later. By then, Allen's career had evolved from stand-up comic to screenwriter. In 1965 he wrote and starred in the comedy *What's New Pussycat?* alongside Peter O'Toole, Peter Sellers and Ursula Andress. He also wrote and starred in the 1969 Broadway hit *Play It Again, Sam*, which brought Diane Keaton to the stage and into Allen's bed. Although they split up after a year, the pair continued to be closely linked

Allen's first wife, teenager Harlene Rosen, whom he cruelly called 'Quasimodo'.

Allen's second marriage to actress Louise Lasser was equally short-lived.

and famously appeared together in the 1977 film *Annie Hall*, which he wrote for her. It secured his reputation by winning four Academy Awards: Best Picture, Best Actress for Keaton, plus Best Screenplay and Best Director for him. What was not mentioned at the Oscars ceremony was the 'bit part' played in *Annie Hall* by actress Stacey Nelkin. Her role ended up on the cutting-room floor but Stacey herself ended up as Allen's young lover, she being 17 and he 42.

It was after this romantic fling ended that Woody Allen began seeing Mia Farrow. The waif-like actress had already made headlines worldwide because of her short-lived 1966 marriage to singer Frank Sinatra, thirty years her senior. Best known for her title role in the critically-acclaimed film *Rosemary's Baby*, Mia's next headline-making event was her 1970 marriage to orchestra conductor André Previn, by whom she already had twin boys. Another son followed before the couple adopted three more children: two Vietnamese infants and a Korean girl. Following her divorce from Previn in 1979, single mother Mia adopted another Korean infant, Moses, who suffered from cerebral palsy.

Mia Farrow had herself been a victim of polio when she was 9 years old and her famously frail, childlike appearance obviously fitted Woody Allen's particular taste in women when he first met her in 1979. The couple began a twelve-year relationship the following year but never married. Neither did they live together, choosing separate apartments in sight of one another across New York's Central Park. Mia wanted children with Woody, who agreed only on the understanding that he need not be fully involved in their care. When efforts to become pregnant failed, however, Farrow adopted a two-week-old girl who she named Dylan. Two years later, the couple managed to have a biological child, initially named Satchel but later known as Ronan. In 1991 Allen also formally adopted two of Mia's children, Moses and Dylan.

Then came the events that blew apart Allen's cosy image. In late 1991, Farrow was at Allen's home when she came across nude pictures of the adopted daughter that she and André Previn had rescued from the slums of the South Korean capital, Seoul. The girl, Soon-Yi Previn, the abandoned daughter of a prostitute, reportedly had learning difficulties and a low IQ. She had always lived with Farrow and had little contact with Allen until 1990 when he suddenly started taking her on outings. Because of her background, Soon-Yi's age has never been firmly ascertained but she is likely to have been 7 years old when adopted in 1978. This made her aged 20 or 21 when Allen, then 56, photographed her

Allen's friend and lover Diane Keaton.

147

naked. Confronted by Mia, Allen admitted taking the photographs, two weeks after he had first had sex with her. He had told his stepdaughter: 'Just lean back and give me your most erotic poses. Let yourself go.' Recoiling in horror and pain at the double betrayal, Farrow engaged lawyers to try to prevent Allen's contact with Soon-Yi but the girl was already infatuated with her stepfather and Allen issued a statement saying they were in love.

Worse was to come. Later that year, Farrow accused Allen of molesting another adopted daughter, Dylan Farrow. The claim, which Dylan has consistently affirmed, was that in August 1992, when she was just 7 years of age, Allen paid a visit to her mother's country home in Connecticut. There, he led her into a 'dim closet-like' attic and told her to lie on her stomach and play with her brother's electric train set. Then, she said, he sexually assaulted her.

This fresh allegation sparked one of the most vitriolic and longest-running domestic battles in Hollywood history: a very public fight between two very private people, during which the weird world of Woody Allen was laid bare. Predictably, the actor-director depicted the child molestation claim as an offshoot of his 'terribly acrimonious break-up' with Farrow. Coming eight months after the revelation of his affair with Soon-Yi, Farrow was accused by him of concocting the story as an act of vengeance, and coaching young Dylan to confirm it.

In a strange response to the allegation, Allen sued Farrow for sole custody of Moses, aged 15, Satchel, aged 5, and Dylan. The resultant court case made headlines worldwide. Allen was depicted as the villain of the piece, while newspapers presented a tortured visage of Farrow, left to care for the rest of her brood alone. Who could blame her when she said: 'I regret the day I ever met him and I hope I never see him again.'

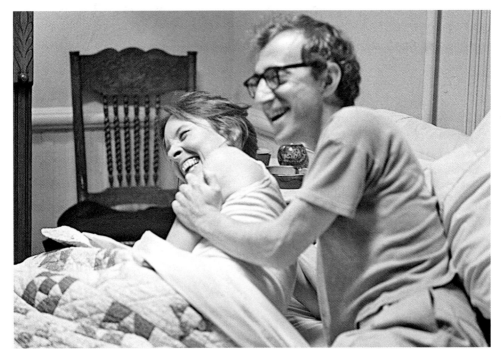

Woody Allen and Diane Keaton joking on the set of their 1977 film *Annie Hall*.

Stacey Nelkin with photos of herself as a teenager bedded by 42-year-old Allen.

Mia Farrow and extended family after her divorce from conductor André Previn.

In court, Allen was portrayed as having little grip on reality, being aloof and stand-offish, patronizing and pompous. He was, at best, an absent father who had little to do with the daily lives of the children he professed to love, even hiring a 'professional shopper' to buy presents for them. Judge Elliott Wilk damned Allen with these words:

> He lacked familiarity with the most basic details of their day-to-day existence. He did not bathe his children. He did not dress them except from time to time and then only to help them put on their socks and jackets. He knows little of Moses' history except that he has cerebral palsy. He does not know if he has a doctor. He does not know the name of Dylan's and Satchel's pediatrician. He does not know the name of Moses' teachers or about his academic performance. He does not know the name of the children's dentist. He does not know the names of his children's friends. He does not know the names of any of their pets.

Judge Wilk ruled that Allen could see his son Satchel for just six hours a week and only then under supervision. He was forbidden to see Dylan at all. An investigation decided there was insufficient evidence to support Mia's child abuse allegations; however, the state's lead prosecutor said there had been 'probable cause' to charge Allen but, in agreement with Farrow, Dylan was considered too 'fragile' to handle a celebrity court case. Instead, the war of words between the protagonists went into overdrive. Mia's fiery lawyer, Eleanor Alter, portrayed Allen as a corrupt, self-obsessed monster who had destroyed Farrow's family in a matter of months. Describing the photographs he took of Soon-Yi as 'pornographic' and 'repulsive', she raged:

> Nobody with regard for women could have taken pictures like that. They show a contempt for Soon-Yi and all women. I mean, this child was a virgin. And she is low-IQ; she is learning-disabled. This is a kid who went to a Catholic school and never had a date. And those pictures! You haven't seen the pictures. I don't know what I would do if I found pictures like that of my child taken by my lover.

Mia and Woody with Dylan Farrow and baby Satchel (later renamed Ronan).

I would either have ended up in a mental institution or I would have killed him.

Mia just worries what will happen to Soon-Yi after Woody dumps her.

That did not happen. In fact, five years after the scandal broke, Woody Allen married Soon-Yi and they subsequently adopted two children of their own. Mia Farrow also continued adding to her family. Between 1992 and 1995, she adopted five more children, one of whom she gave the name 'Wilk' after the judge in the case. Farrow said: 'You become very strong when your children are threatened. I've been to Hell and back. I dug deep and found hidden reserves in myself that I never knew existed.'

In the ongoing battle between the two factions, Dylan's brother Moses backed his father, claiming that Farrow had created 'an atmosphere of fear and hate' among the children and had coached them to believe falsely that Allen had molested Dylan. However, her brother Ronan has always supported her story, saying: 'I believe my sister.'

Woody Allen always maintained that adverse media attention had not dented his career nor subjected him to public hostility. Perhaps the biggest horror for him was to have had his private world dissected but he endured it, he said, for the sake of his children: 'I don't like publicity or interviews and nobody likes to be falsely accused of a crime. But when my children get older, I want them to know that their father didn't abandon them but gave it his all.'

Allen holds Dylan Farrow in 1987.

Such optimism was unsustainable, however, as other film stars and financiers finally began to turn their backs on Allen. It had taken more than a quarter of a century but Dylan's claims at last found a sympathetic hearing in Hollywood following a storm of other sexual abuse allegations against powerful figures such as movie mogul Harvey Weinstein and actor Kevin Spacey. By then aged 32, Dylan appeared on a 2018 American TV programme in which she was played an old tape of her stepfather protesting his innocence. She burst into tears, saying: 'I'm sorry. I thought I could handle it. It's difficult to see him and to hear his voice. He's lying and he's been lying for so long.'

Mia and Woody in 1991, the year he formally adopted two of her children, Moses and Dylan.

Allen with Soon-Yi. They married in 1997 and subsequently adopted two children of their own.

Claims by Dylan Farrow (left) that Allen abused her were backed by her brother Ronan (right).

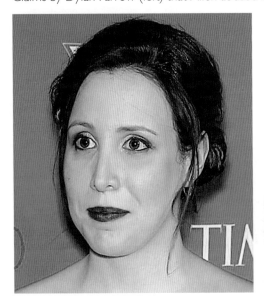